The Clay Canvas

The Clay Canvas

Creative Painting on Functional Ceramics

Irene Wittig

Chilton Book Company
Radnor, Pennsylvania

Designed by Gloria Gentile for Spectrum Publisher Services
Manufactured in the United States of America

Library of Congress Cataloging in Publication Data

Wittig, Irene.
    The clay canvas : creative painting on functional ceramics / Irene
Wittig.
        p.   cm.
    Includes index.
    ISBN 0-8019-8016-X (pbk.)
    1. China painting.   I. Title.
NK4605.W63   1991
738.1′5—dc20   90-55327
                                                       CIP

1 2 3 4 5 6 7 8 9 0   9 8 7 6 5 4 3 2 1

To Joan Coffey O'Connor

Grace was in all her steps, heaven in her eye,
In every gesture dignity and love.

John Milton

Contents

Acknowledgments

To Wayne,
my husband and dearest friend, for his unlimited help, encouragement, patience, good ideas and good humor.

To Caitlin,
my daughter, for her happy laughter, willing help and artistic advice; for her delicious chocolate chip cookies; and for letting me use her work in this book.

To Timothy,
my son, for keeping me on my toes with jokes, card tricks and ambushes—and for the chance to include his work in this book.

To Diane Herbort,
my neighbor and friend, for her invaluable advice and generosity. It was inspiring to have access to her innumerable artistic ideas—as well as all her books, cards, fabrics, paints, magic markers, etc.

To David Allison,
for his skillful and patient photography. It's a grand feeling to think that my work has joined the private art collections, Smithsonian artifacts and archival documents that he usually photographs.

To Donna Cantor,
for the thrill of my first professional photographs.

To Terry Millar,
an installer of tiles with eyes of an artist.

To MJ Designs Craft Supplies,
for the kind loan of flowers.

To Rosemary Maceiras, of *McCalls Needlework and Crafts Magazine,*
for making my first publishing experiences so enjoyable.

To Montage of Georgetown in Washington, D.C.,
for being just the shop I was looking for.

Introduction: The Delights of a Clay Canvas

I fell head over heels in love with the colorful handpainted ceramics of southern Italy when we lived in Naples. Sitting on our balcony, drinking coffee out of cups splashed with handpainted flowers, I often looked out over the bay and pictured the little ceramic factories along the coast that had become so familiar to us. And there, right under Mount Vesuvius, I could almost see the shop of Signor Deo.

Signor Deo was an elderly gentleman who owned a little ceramic shop in the industrial town of San Giovanni, half-way between Naples and Pompeii. I discovered his talents through a friend who was working at an orphanage nearby. Signor Deo, she told me with delight, didn't just sell ceramics; he was an artist who painted on tiles. He painted scenes from his imagination or yours. I was enchanted and found myself buying his paintings for everyone—scenes of the hillside houses of Capri, of terracotta pots overflowing with flowers, of alpine villages. I visited often, watching him work in a little corner at the back of his shop. I asked many questions. The colors he used were unrecognizable and indistinguishable from each other until they were glazed and fired. How could he predict his results so well? It just takes practice he said.

I didn't think of practicing for myself at that time. I was intimidated by those mystery colors. Besides, it didn't seem necessary. I was surrounded by an abundance of inexpensive and wonderful, colorful, handpainted ceramics. My husband and I spent many a day browsing through the ceramic factories in Vietri and the shops along the Amalfi coast. As we traveled around Italy, we admired the variety of styles we found. We bought many presents, of course. For ourselves we chose the more unique and contemporary pieces. But when we were back in the United States we realized that we really missed the magic and the art of the everyday ceramics of southern Italy. We should have brought home more of those traditional pieces that had seemed so common then. At first, I thought it would be easy enough to find them here too. But it wasn't. I craved some colorful, handpainted little mugs to hold my espresso and feed my nostalgia.

Then one day, a couple of years later, I happened to talk to a ceramist who had worked for Wheaton Glass in its now-defunct china factory in Millville, New Jersey, and now ran its discount outlet store. In the store she had set up a small ceramic workshop where she decorated and sold the unglazed bisqueware left over from the factory. I still pined for some handpainted mugs and asked her how she decorated the bisque, remembering Signor Deo's mystery colors. Unlike Signor Deo, she used concentrated, one-stroke underglazes, which look unglazed much like they look glazed and fired. I was thrilled at this discovery.

"Just take this bisque mug, and paint on it with these underglazes. Then glaze and fire it," she said. She left out a couple of steps, I was to discover, but the door had been opened. In short order I had my mugs, painted with my own interpretation of those remembered Italian designs. Soon I had to do some for my friends; after which my friends had me paint mugs, bowls and plates for their friends. One asked if I could do something special for someone who made delicate cloth sculptures of flying animals. I painted a platter of my own design on which her mythological creatures danced. And so it was that, within a year of making my little mugs, I was in business! Although my first pieces were simple and my brushstrokes a bit unpracticed, the more I did the easier it got. And the more I did the more ideas I had. The ideas were the best part.

But things aren't made up of only best parts. After my initial conversation with the ceramist in New Jersey, I found specific information and answers to questions hard to obtain. I didn't quite fit into any category: I wasn't a potter, and I wasn't doing the usual hobby ceramics. I wasn't even considered a craftsperson, because I didn't handcraft the pieces. Painters painted on canvases of cloth or paper. Craftspeople and artists, afraid that their ideas will be stolen, are often reluctant to share techniques except under the protective umbrella of a guild or artists' group. There was no easily identifiable group for me to join, and I'm not an especially eager joiner anyway. What I really wanted and needed was somewhere to go for technical advice, and someone to share ideas with. Then suddenly I found both: first a friendly ceramic shop to help with technical problems, and then Diane Herbort, an innovative needlework and quilt designer, who was kind enough to move in next door. Diane has been endlessly generous with her ideas, her books, her supplies, and most important, her time. With this book I would like to return the favor, since not everyone can have a Diane next door.

If you are thinking that there are already many imaginative handpainted ceramics available—made in Italy, France, Portugal and Mexico, for instance—that you can (and should!) place in every room of your house, remember that they can't compete with the ones you'll make yourself.

Those of you who think you can't paint will find that painting on ceramics with underglazes is an art accessible to everyone. It is much less intimidating than oil or watercolor painting; easier, quicker and more spontaneous than china painting. Although it is hard to correct painting mistakes, it is actually a very forgiving medium. Precision in painting is just a style, not a requirement. Primitiveness can add to the charm. There are no restrictions on your designs. Abstracts, floral, realistic, naive—all of them will work. You are under no pressure to be "an artist with a message." Decorative art will do just fine. Tole painters will take to this medium with no trouble at all, having already found beauty in painting ordinary objects. Children seem instinctively to understand all the possibilities, and take to the medium eagerly. They take great pride in seeing their pictures become permanent and not just refrigerator pin-up art.

If you are a hobby-ceramist or potter, you will discover that free-hand, creative painting on ceramics will add an extra dimension to your work. Hobby-ceramists, you don't need to limit yourself to items that end up merely as knickknacks. Don't just follow paint-by-number type of instructions, paying little attention to the many possibilities of real surface design, and thinking "I'm not an artist." Potters, you need not concentrate only on form and shape, satisfying yourselves with neutral glazes, because you think "I'm not a painter."

Painters, this is also a splendid new outlet for you. Don't feel restricted to 11" × 14" sheets of paper, or 2' × 3' canvases, and overlook the "fine art" possibilities of combining art, color, form and function on a clay canvas. It will also solve the problem of what to do with all those pictures! Now you can have canvases that can be used as well as looked at. In fact it is their very usefulness that makes them so appealing. The combination of beauty and practicality makes art seem approachable and understandable. As the ever-popular English Country Style can testify, plates and bowls, teapots and cups, vases and boxes make wonderful decoration in any room. From kitchen to bedroom, their presence graciously invites us to use them. A room can hardly seem cold or impersonal if it is filled with things lovingly made.

We have experienced a revival of interest in arts and crafts in recent years. But in the desire to raise crafts to art, we often sacrificed their significance as accessories of our daily life. What is considered art by many is too often limited to high-priced, non-functional items to be looked at and admired from a distance. We have often settled for generic art: mass-produced, impersonal design. Somehow we have let our everyday be separated from a sense of art.

I would like, with this book, to do my part to return art to the accessories and tools of daily life. To add artistic expression to the articles of our everyday, we need to add personal expression to the things we use and with which we surround ourselves. We have many historical examples for this. Artisans, soldiers, farmers, fishermen saw dignity in the tools that provided them with their livelihood and identities, and made these tools objects deserving of art and ornamentation. Women, honoring the symbols of their occupations, wove, embroidered, or quilted linens and clothing, creating art and memories. And thus ordinary people became extraordinary, for they created things that would connect future generations to their past better than any history lesson. After all, aren't museums filled with their handiwork?

These clay canvases, that I am so eager for you to discover, are easily available to you and will let you express your ideas of beauty and design. They will also let you translate important times, people and places into pictures you can touch and hold in your hands. One doesn't expect the personal on objects that are purchased. Handpainted ceramics will become your bridge between the homemade and the manufactured and a wonderful means to personalizing your environment. You will be able to create designs that complement colors and patterns in your home. You will be able to capture life's moments, and people dear to you, on the objects you use and surround yourself with. Grandma Moses, in painting her memories of people and places important to her, created not only art but social history. Ceramics are a wonderful medium for these reminiscences and commemorations. The interaction of the two-dimensional decoration and the three-dimensional form and shape adds an element of discovery and involvement. Your work becomes something to handle, with fingers reading the details. Your favorite pieces will take on the comfortable familiarity of a handknit sweater.

When given as a gift, a handpainted ceramic piece can be just the beginning instead of a one-time event. It is hard to give someone a whole series of paintings (unless you are Monet, of course). But there is something lovely about adding to a set of handpainted dishes year after year.

In the following chapters I will explain what you need to have and to do to be a ceramic painter. I start with a general description of the ceramic process, and a detailed description of equipment you would need to do all of it. This will help you decide how much of the process you would like to do yourself. Familiarity with the terms will also make the subsequent how-to chapter easy to understand. You can start small—only a few materials are needed for the painting.

Chapter 6 contains several projects to help you get started, but from experience I know that your own ideas will tumble out in great abundance once you've painted your first pieces. Enjoy it and spread the word. Soon you will have a large network of fellow enthusiasts with whom to share ideas and techniques.

1

*O*ne of the practical aspects of painting on ceramics is that you can choose to do as much or as little of the whole ceramic process as you wish. It's somewhat like making a birthday cake. The cake needs making, baking and decorating. You can buy the ingredients and make it from scratch, use a mix, or buy a finished cake, and decorate any one of them. The same thing applies to handpainted ceramics. The piece needs to be made, painted and fired.

Who performs the various steps of the ceramic process is up to you. To help you decide, let's see what the different steps entail, and the pros and cons of doing them yourself.

Making the Piece

Pieces can be hand-formed out of clay, thrown on a wheel or slipcast (i.e., liquid clay, called slip, is poured into molds). See Fig. 1-1. Because some of the colors (underglazes) change or even fade out at high firing temperatures, you will have the broadest range of colors at your disposal if you use articles made of low-fire clay (i.e., earthenware rather than the high-fire stoneware or porcelain). Slipcast

FIG. 1-1 Clay articles can be hand-formed (vase), thrown (bowl) or slipcast (watering can). The vase was hand-formed by my daughter. The bowl was thrown and decorated by Washington, D.C., potter Susan Jacobs. *Photo by David Allison*

ware is usually of low-fire clay. Although there is true pleasure in making your own articles out of solid clay, slipcast ware lends itself very well to painting with great opportunity for creativity. To cast your own molds is a big job and requires a lot of space and equipment, so I will assume that you will purchase slipcast ware made by someone else. Normally slipcast pieces are sold unfired as greenware. Though called "green" because they are "uncooked," they are actually gray in color. Greenware needs to be cleaned and then fired to bisque. Bisque, the term for fired but unglazed clay, is then ready for painting.

Greenware

Cleaning

Assuming you are buying slipcast greenware, the first decision will be who "cleans" the greenware. Cleaning means smoothing out all rough areas and seams so as to prepare the surfaces for painting., Cleaning is not difficult. It requires very little equipment and not much space, but it is a bit messy and not thrilling. You may decide to ask your local ceramic shop to do this and pay for their labor.

Firing

Firing is the "baking" step. Your piece will be fired at least three times: to remove moisture and organic matter from the greenware and turn it into bisque; to set the colors after you've painted and prevent them from smearing; and to fire the glaze and create a glass-like surface finish. To be able to fire, a safe space with adequate ventilation is needed for a kiln. If you live in an apartment you would probably prefer taking your pieces to a ceramic shop to be fired. Community centers and schools often have kilns you can use.

If you have someone else do the firing, you have one job less and need less space and equipment. However, if you do your own firing you will save quite a lot of money in the long run, and will have more control over your pieces and your time.

Painting a Ceramic Piece

This is the main point, of course, and the most enjoyable and creative part so there is no doubt you will be doing it. For this you need only brushes and under-glazes. They don't take up much space, and neither do you and the piece you are painting, so you can paint anywhere. I started working at my kitchen counter. Then as my hobby, and later my business, grew I expanded into the dining room. Only after I had built up a fairly large inventory of bisque, supplies and reference materials did I need a work room of my own.

If you have none of the materials mentioned, then you can begin with just those needed to paint, and ask your ceramic shop to do the rest. Cleaning green-

FIG. 1-2 Although there are many tools available, the only ones you will need to clean your greenware are nylon scrubbing pads (one smoother than the other), a sponge and a double spiral brush. *Photo by David Allison*

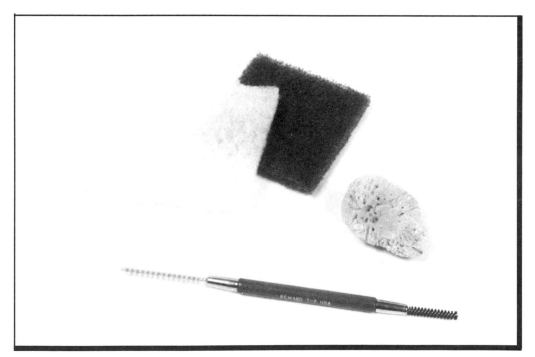

ware and glazing are easy and require few materials, so you can soon try them too. Then when you find yourself full of ideas and looking forward to your next project, you can start thinking about investing in a kiln. Shopping for such accoutrements and specialized products is one of the pleasures of a hobby, after all.

I have divided this list of required equipment and materials into the three phases of production: cleaning greenware, painting and firing. I have assumed, in developing this list, that you have no materials at all. So don't panic at the length of the list! You don't need everything at once. And if you already have done ceramics and have tools of your own that you find satisfactory, you probably don't need to get others. If you are a painter in another medium, you can use many of your brushes on this medium too. (Just make sure they are completely clean.)

Equipment Needed for Cleaning Greenware

Greenware needs to be cleaned of all rough areas, nicks and seams. There are many tools available, but I find these few are the only ones I really need and are the easiest to use. See Fig. 1-2.

Nylon Cleaning Pads
Green (Coarse), White (Fine)
They wear out quickly, so have several on hand. Don't be tempted to get Scotch-Brite pads, for although they look similar, they are for scrubbing pots and pans and are too coarse for this work.

Sponge
The softest is a natural sea sponge. Use this for final smoothing and removing dust.

Double Spiral Brush
This looks like a small bottle brush with spiral on each end. Good for cleaning undersides and insides of handles.

Brushes

This phase is the most fun to buy for, as most painters will already know. There's real pleasure in buying a perfect brush or finding a wonderful new color!

Ceramic supply companies manufacture their own line of brushes, but you can also use regular artists' brushes. The important things to look for are good bristles that form good points. Ceramic painting is harder on brushes than other painting because bisque is rougher and more porous than paper or canvas. First decide what kind of brushstrokes you will need to make and then look for appropriate brushes of good quality. See Fig. 1-3. In the following paragraphs I have listed the sizes and types that I find the most useful. Don't be afraid to experiment, you

FIG. 1-3 Detail brushes are on the left, then liners, rounds and flats. The large brushes at right are for glazing, but can be used for painting, too. *Photo by David Allison*

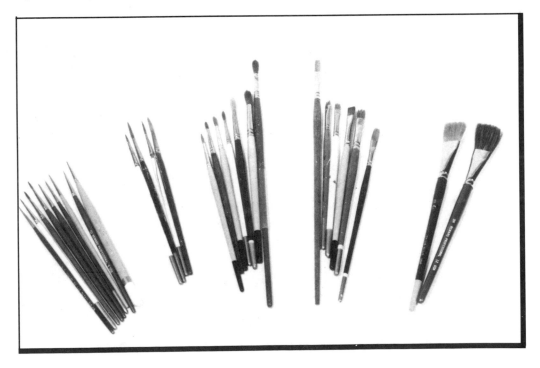

may discover your own favorites. The next chapter will explain how these brushes are used and will show you sample strokes.

Liner Brushes

Buy two sizes: one fine (size 1 or 2), and one fuller (size 3 or 4). Red sable is the best quality. Good for flowing lines with varying thicknesses. Use for ribbons, long leaves, tendrils and script.

Round Brush

Buy sable or sabeline, size 4. For pressure strokes and larger areas of coverage. Good for petals and leaves as well as other shapes.

Detail Brush

Buy size 0, 1 and/or 2. This is probably the brush I use the most: for details, lettering, small area coverage and outlining. It can often take the place of the liner brush, except for long, flowing lines. This is also the brush I replace the most often. Try to stock up on these since the point gets a lot of use, and becomes ragged on bisque. Small brushes are less expensive than large ones, so this is not as bad as it sounds. Shop around and try different brands and sizes. Some brands are cheaper by the dozen.

Flat Bristle $\frac{1}{4}''$

I like the long bristled white sable. The flat portion is usable for broad coverage and washes; and its chisel point can be used for both lines and pressure strokes.

Glaze Brush $\frac{3}{4}''$ or $1''$

I like to use a flat brush, but you can also use the fuller mop brush. Your main concern here is that the brush not shed bristles, for they can get stuck in the wet glaze.

Sponges

These can also be used to apply underglazes. They work especially well on borders, or to indicate leaves or grass as seen from a distance. Try not to use your cleaning sponge for applying underglazes, unless you clean thoroughly.

Underglazes

Underglazes are the colors with which you will paint. They come in liquid (in jars), semi-moist (in pans or tubes) and dry (as pencils or crayons). See Fig. 1-4. Covered with a non-toxic, food-safe glaze, the painted surface will be safe for holding food. Some underglazes are opaque, some are translucent. Some require three coats, some only one; and one line of colors can be used both ways. In general, the colors are in harmony and work well together as a family. Most of them are not brilliant, even if strong. I have not found a true red that is easy to use, so I substitute rose and cranberry shades.

One-Stroke Concentrated Translucent Underglazes

These highly concentrated colors look and work somewhat like watercolors. They can be applied one over the other for shading. Light colors over dark won't work as well, of course, as dark colors over light. Because the bisque surface is more porous than paper and absorbs the "paint" more quickly, you won't be able to create smooth, flowing washes as easily as you could on paper.

One-Stroke Concentrated Opaque Underglazes and Multi-Coat Opaque Underglazes

If you don't want streaking, or a see-through quality, or want to create highlights with light colors on top of dark then you can use one-stroke opaque underglazes. For larger opaque areas use opaque underglazes that require two or three strokes. One brand of underglazes (Duncan's Design Coats) can be diluted for a semi-opaque effect, or used full strength (one or more coats) for opaque or larger area coverage. Detail work will be easier with concentrated colors because of the thinner consistency of the colors.

In addition to translucency or opacity, there is one other consideration in deciding which of the underglazes to use. The one-stroke translucent underglazes look, on bisque, more or less how they will look once they are glazed and fired. Some colors will darken, and others (primarily reds and yellows that are too diluted) can fade out in firing, but you can plan color combinations easily. The three-stroke opaque underglazes, on the other hand, often look alike and nothing like they will

FIG. 1-4   Some of the underglaze materials that you can use to decorate and paint on your clay canvases. Pencils can be used to create sketch and charcoal effects. Crayons apply and look like pastels. Semi-moist and liquid underglazes can be translucent or opaque and apply like paints.   *Photo by David Allison*

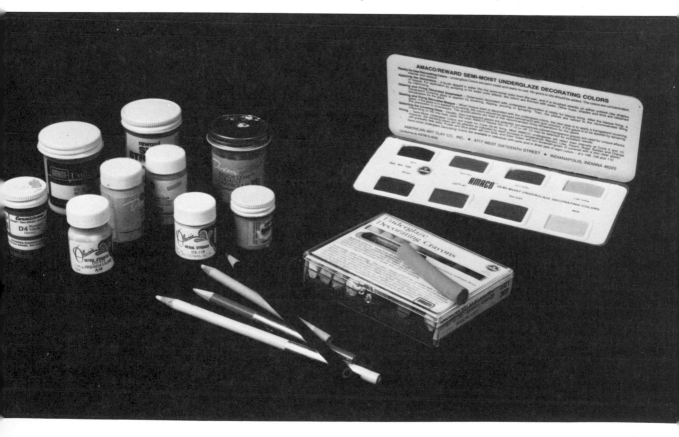

later (Signor Deo's mystery colors)! You will have to imagine the color results in
your mind. This is not difficult if you are doing just one or two large areas, using
flesh tones, or just putting in a few touches. It is more difficult to imagine your
results if you are using a wide variety of colors, or planning a complex design using
only these underglazes.

Underglaze Pencils

To create the effect of sketching or to draw soft outlines use underglaze pencils. They
come in several colors, but I find black and brown the most useful. Red and yellow
tend to fade out too easily.

Glazes

Glazes are applied over the painted ceramic surface and fired to form a glass-
like, protective coating. Once glazed and fired, underglazes are permanent and can
no longer fade or chip. There are many glazes in many colors and textures. The
only one you'll need is a food-safe clear, gloss (shiny) glaze. Applied correctly, it will
make the ceramic surface impermeable, and safe to eat from and put food into.
You can buy it by the gallon and save a lot of money.

Gold and Silver Overglazes

Gold or silver can be added as overglazes. This is to be done only on works
that will not come into contact with food or drink (and therefore mouths). I use it
rarely, but when I do I use a gold or silver pen. It works like a fine point felt-tip pen, is
easy to use and seems to have a long shelf life. Gold is expensive, and this is a
method that has little waste. This overglaze needs to be fired on.

Miscellaneous Materials

An Old Margarine Tub in Which to Put the Glaze
A Jar of Fresh Water (Replace Water Often)
Paper Towels

Equipment Needed for Firing

You don't need to invest in this phase when you first begin. There are many ceramic studios, public schools and recreation centers that can do your firing. Once you are in love with this new medium, you will not want to waste time and money taking things out to be fired, so then you can invest in an electric kiln. See Fig. 1-5.

Fig. 1-5 A medium-sized 220 volt electric kiln will fill your needs for a long time.

Photo courtesy of Duncan Enterprises

Electric Kiln

You will find an electric kiln pays for itself very quickly. Kilns come in many sizes. You can start with a very small one. It has the advantage of being able to fire just one or two pieces at a time, and is usually 110 volt so that it can be used along with any other household appliance (with proper ventilation). But, if you are ready to invest in a kiln it probably means you are also ready to do more work and need a larger kiln. My own kiln has a firing chamber (interior dimensions) that is $17\frac{1}{2}''$ wide by $19\frac{1}{2}''$ deep, and I have found that to be sufficient for almost all my needs. On the rare occasions I need something bigger, I take my work out to a ceramic shop to be fired.

NOTE: Before deciding on a kiln ask yourself the following questions.

How big a kiln do I really need? This will depend on how much work you do at one time, and how big the pieces usually are. If you do a lot of dinnerware, for instance, then a kiln of my size is important. Plates take up a lot of horizontal space and platters even more. If you want to do only mugs, or Christmas ornaments, or other small pieces once in a while, then the smallest kiln would be fine. Don't underestimate the size you need, but don't overestimate either. A very large kiln takes long to heat up and long to cool down, and of course, uses more electricity.

Do I have space for it? Can I put it somewhere where proper ventilation is possible?

Do I have or can I get 220 volt capability and the proper wiring? Only the small kiln can run on 110 volts.

Before choosing a specific brand or model do some research. Find out what kiln dealers in your area can do repair work. Although some kiln repairs are actually quite simple, you just never know.

Ask about safety and energy-saving features. I highly recommend having a kiln sitter as well as an automatic timer/shut-off switch. They can spare you unfortunate over-firings and misfirings.

Before buying a kiln, check if there are any hobby ceramic shows coming up. Dealers sell at close to wholesale prices there and often have specials. Shows are also great places to stock up on glaze and brushes. Brushes are often sold by the dozen at great savings. But be sure you know your brushes. You certainly don't want twelve brushes that don't work!

Kiln Furniture and Accessories

There's also some equipment you will need for the kiln. See Fig. 1-6. Usually if there is a special price on the kiln there will be a special on kiln furniture kits too. This is what you will need.

FIG. 1-6 Kiln furniture includes shelves (a half-shelf is pictured), shelf supports of different heights, a variety of stilts to hold glazed articles, and a pyrometric cone and bar.

Photo by David Allison

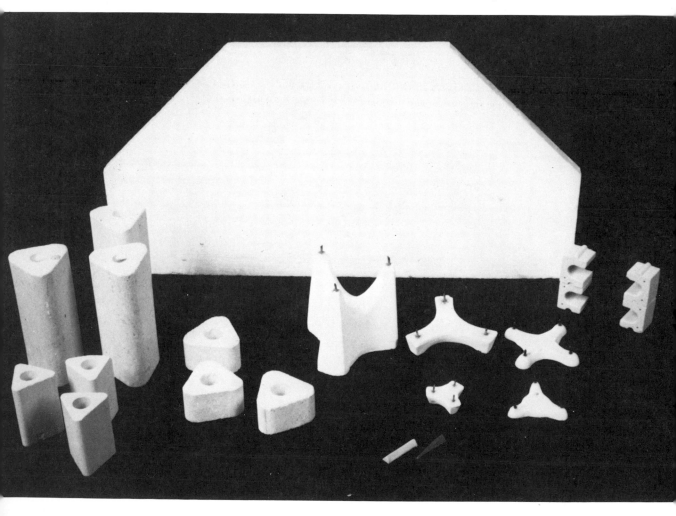

Kiln Shelves

I have six shelves and two half-shelves for my size kiln because I paint a lot of tiles and plates. One shelf is placed and stays on the bottom of the kiln as protection.

Kiln Wash

This is a coating for the bottom of the kiln and for the top side of the shelves to protect them from glaze drippings. It is not expensive and is easy to brush on.

Posts

Posts are the supports for the shelves. Their height determines how far apart the shelves are, so you want an assortment of sizes. You need three supports to hold up a shelf. You can stack the posts to make taller supports. I suggest having the following sizes (and remember, at least three of each size): $\frac{1}{2}''$, 1", 2", 3", 5" and 6". The taller ones provide better support if they are also wider in diameter.

Stilts

Stilts are used to hold up your glazed pieces so that they don't touch the shelves and stick to them when they are fired. They come in many sizes; the sizes you need are determined by the pieces you make. Generally $1\frac{1}{2}''$, 2" and 3" three-legged stilts will fit most needs.

Pyrometric Cones

Cones act as heat-measuring devices. They are a composite of special clays that bend when the kiln reaches a specific temperature. Just when this happens depends on the rate at which you are firing (how fast you turn up the temperature), how high you turn up the kiln, how big the kiln is and how full. When the cone bends it triggers the kiln sitter which then shuts off the kiln. And in case that doesn't work— which has been known to happen—you should also have the safety timer/shut-off switch that will turn off the kiln at a time you have specified. The cone designations indicate specific temperature ranges. So if it is recommended that a glaze be fired to cone 06, that means fire the kiln until the 06 cone bends. The small cones used in *kiln sitters are generally available from designations cone 022 (low) to cone 8 (high), but our purposes will need only 06 and 04 cones—and cone 018 if you are adding gold with a pen. These cones correspond approximately as follows to specific temperatures:*

Cone 018 = 720° C or 1330° F
Cone 06 = 1015° C or 1860° F
Cone 04 = 1060° C or 1940° F

I find the bar-shaped firing cones easier to use and less fragile than the tapered ones. The tapered ones can trip the kiln sitter earlier or later, depending on whether the thick or the thin part of the cone is under the sensing rod.

Stilt Stone
A stilt stone is used to remove stilt marks and drips from a finished piece. You will probably want this even if you don't do your own firing; and you will probably need only one in your life.

2

"What Do I Do and How Do I Do It?"

*A*fter reading Chapter 1, you may have already decided whether you will concentrate on painting or whether you prefer a more total-craftsman approach. Your preference may be determined by how much space you can give to it. It is probably wisest to start small and then expand. Whatever you decide, for purposes of this book I will assume that at some time you will want to know how to do it all: clean, paint, glaze and fire.

Practicing Before Beginning: Making Color Swatches

Before you get into choosing a more elaborate project, you should practice. Tiles are great for this. You can buy hand-cast tiles at a ceramic shop and have the chance to practice easy cleaning on greenware, or you can buy a quantity of less expensive tiles, already fired to bisque, from a tile supply house. Whether you are a beginner or an experienced painter you will want to practice your brushstrokes on this new medium. You'll find that although the bisque surface absorbs colors more quickly than paper or canvas, you will soon feel comfortable with it. You'll want to try out all your brushes and the various strokes that they can create.

Try out all the colors you have too, as you go along. Have at least one or two of each kind of underglaze (one-stroke, three-stroke, translucent and opaque) so that you can try out how they feel under your hand. Some people will prefer thicker colors, larger brushes and broader strokes, whereas others will feel more at ease using light, delicate strokes and thinner colors. Group the colors as you paint them, putting blues together in one group, greens in another and so on. You can identify them by number or name, practicing your alphabet strokes as you write with the detail brush. Or you can write with the underglaze pencil. On other tiles, experiment with how one color works over another.

After you've finished these practice tiles, make sure to glaze them and have them fired so that you can see what changes take place. Keep these color swatches for you'll find them to be much more useful than color charts printed on paper. You may find it helpful to read the section on "Painting with Underglazes" on page 30 before you start practicing.

Choosing a Project

You now have to decide what article to make and what design you would like to put on it. Chapters 4 and 5 go into this fully, and Chapter 6 provides you with specific project ideas and designs. You will find it helpful to read and understand these how-tos before you choose your own project. Remember to start simply for it will help you gain confidence. Most ceramic shops have a wide variety of molds from which you should choose a piece that is simple in shape and has smooth surfaces to work on. Avoid articles with designs already molded in or onto them, as they will limit the amount of painting surface you have. As you get more expert you can consider pre-molded designs if they contribute to your ideas. If you make your own piece, be sure to use low-fire clay and not porcelain or stoneware.

Your practice piece will be a small plate. You can choose one with or without a rim.

Preparing the Greenware

Clean your greenware as soon as you buy it. The longer it sits, the harder the dry clay becomes and the more difficult it is to smooth down. It is very important to *handle greenware carefully.* It is only dry clay and will break if you put too much pressure on it. It can't handle much weight, so don't hold cups by the handles. And don't squeeze. The fragility of the greenware is one reason I like to fire it to bisque before I paint. Make sure your hands are free of oil, lotion or salt since they could affect glazes applied later.

Take the coarser nylon cleaning pad, the green one, and remove the roughest areas by rubbing across them. Remember to be gentle even if you are scrubbing. After removing the seam lines and especially rough areas, move the pad in a circular motion to further smooth the surface and remove imperfections. The simpler and flatter the surface, the easier it will be to clean. You will find that these green pads wear out quickly because of the rough surfaces of the clay.

Follow this cleaning with the finer white nylon pad and continue smoothing all the surfaces, using the same circular motions. These pads will last longer because they meet less resistance.

If there are areas that are hard to reach, like the underside of cup handles, use the two-ended spiral brush.

Blow off excess dust, then gently smooth down the greenware surface with a damp sponge. This will also remove the dust. Sponge gently, for if you are pressing too hard you will rub off more clay and create more dust. Fig. 2-1 shows a slipcast piece before and after cleaning.

Special instructions for your practice piece: Hold the plate carefully, with fingers under the center of the plate and thumb against the side or on top. Don't hold the plate by the rim—it may break off.

Follow the cleaning procedures described in this section. The roughest areas of a hand-cast plate are usually the edge and sometimes the bottom.

FIG. 2-1 Two slipcast mugs in the greenware stage. The one on the left has not been "cleaned," whereas the one on the right has had all seams and rough areas smoothed down. It is now ready to fire to bisque.   *Photo by David Allison*

First Firing: Bisque

Bisque is the term for fired, unglazed clay. Hard bisque is fired to cone 04 or higher, medium bisque to cone 05 and soft bisque to cone 06. (NOTE: the higher the number with a zero in front of it, the lower the temperature; the higher the number without a zero in front of it, the higher the temperature—therefore, cone 6 is much hotter than cone 06, and cone 04 is hotter than cone 05. For an analogy, think of a thermometer with the "zero" ratings as minus temperatures and the "non-zero" ratings as plus temperatures.) The two advantages of working on bisque rather than greenware are: the bisque firing has baked the clay so that it is not so fragile, and handles and stores more easily; the colors you are applying are easier to judge on the white bisque than on the gray greenware.

Loading the Kiln

Greenware should be placed directly on the shelves without stilts. Try to place the pieces evenly throughout so that the kiln is not more densely loaded in one section than another. This will prevent uneven firing. Greenware still has a lot of water in it. The first firing removes the moisture as well as organic matter. A correctly loaded kiln will ensure even distribution of moisture as well as heat. Lids should be fired on their containers so that if they shrink, they will shrink the same and will fit. The resulting bisque will be dry and very porous. Do not fire greenware with glazed articles because the moisture will affect the glaze. (Don't worry, you won't forget, for you'll be firing them at different temperatures.)

Determining Time and Temperature

You want to make hard bisque, so fire to cone 04. Place the small pyrometric cone in the kiln sitter. Keep the peepholes open to allow oxygen to enter the kiln. (Oxygen is needed to burn out the organic materials in the clay and glazes.) How long the kiln will fire depends on how much greenware is in the kiln and how "fast" you fire it. Since there is so much moisture in the greenware, start the firing slowly (on low), leaving it at low for one hour. Turn to medium for about an hour, and then to high for the rest of the time. This allows the released moisture to escape steadily. The kiln sitter will trigger the shut-off when the kiln reaches the cone 04 temperature. If you have the kiln very full of greenware you might start off with the lid propped open slightly to release some of the moisture, and/or increase the time on low to two hours. If you are using a very small kiln and just have one or two small items, you can work faster and it will need to fire a much shorter time. Whichever kiln you use, let the temperature rise gradually and uniformly. The greenware can explode if it is heated too quickly.

Unloading the Kiln

Let the kiln cool about twice as long as it fired before opening. The top of the kiln should feel cool. If the kiln is opened too soon the clay pieces can break. Open the lid and let the heat out and the cooler air in before unloading. Then you can unload. The bisque is now ready for decorating.

> **Special instructions for your practice piece: Following the procedures just described, fire this piece to cone 04 and remove when cool.**

Sketching the Design

The bisque surface is your canvas. You can sketch on it with pencil, change your mind and erase it—it does not have to be perfect. Don't worry about smudges, they will all burn off in the next firing. Draw lightly, not pressing too hard, so as not to scratch the surface. You will want the sketch to serve as a guideline for your brushstrokes and not as an outline to be filled with color as in a coloring book. Remember, too, that since the pencil marks burn off you do not have to sketch in every small detail. Try not to be tempted to just trace and transfer from a design someone else has developed, for you will enjoy your own efforts much more. If you are convinced that you definitely belong to the "I know I can't draw" faction just start with an abstract design. Squiggles, doodles and blotches can look wonderful in color! And they are a great way to practice brushstrokes and experiment with colors and color composition. Think of it as pure design. You'll still want to use your pencil to mark out basic patterns.

Then when you feel more comfortable, and therefore, more confident, try drawing something free-hand. Start with something simple. You can copy other drawings, but add your own touches and feel free to make changes. Practice really does make perfect, and the more you draw, the easier it becomes. Soon you will find it easier to draw free-hand than to trace. If you are already an experienced painter in another medium, you'll just be adapting to a new medium.

To help divide a plate or platter into sections, use an easy-to-make template. Trace the outline of the piece on a sheet of paper or tracing paper. Cut out the shape. Fold it in half, and again in half, to subdivide the area evenly. This is especially useful for placing repeating elements of a border design. See Fig. 2-2.

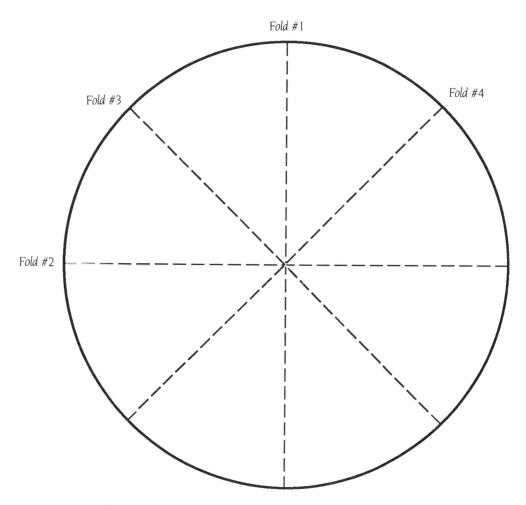

Fig. 2-2 A template for dividing a plate into even sections. This is valuable when you are using a repeat motif, especially on the border. The first fold divides the plate in half; the second, into quarters. The third and fourth folds divide the plate into eighths, etc.

Though I really encourage you to draw freehand as much as possible, there is a time and place for everything. I will let you in on how to trace and transfer a design.

1. With a felt tip pen, trace the desired design on tracing paper.

2. If the design is not the right size, use a copy machine to reduce or enlarge it. If you want it reversed, turn the tracing paper over and make another tracing. You can select different tracings to create a combination design, using a copy machine to put them all on one piece of paper.

3. Place the final design on the top side of the transfer paper (also known as carbon paper and available at ceramic shops and art supply stores), and then place both of them on the bisque with the "carbon" side facing down.

4. Retrace the design with a pencil or pen. The transfer paper acts like carbon paper, and transfers the design onto the bisque. Or:

5. Rub your pencil on the back of the tracing paper, carbonizing the surface. Then retrace the design and transfer it onto the bisque.

> **Special instructions for your practice piece: Looking at the example in Fig. 2-3, sketch your own version, making changes or additions. This can be a birthday plate with name, date, a floral border and a baby chick design in the center. You can sign it and write "Love . . ." on the back. I have used my daughter's name on the finished plate (see color section).**

Painting with Underglazes

This is the part that seems the hardest to those who are new to painting. But "Don't worry, be happy," as they say, for this is also the part that is the most fun and the most creative. You will find it much easier than you think. First I'll tell you about the colors and underglazes, and then about the brushes. Finally you can try them out as you paint a birthday plate.

Colors

Although you can paint in just one or two colors (remember blue and white Delftware?), I find the freshest and friendliest designs arise from using more colors.

FIG. 2-3 Guideline drawing for your practice piece. You can copy it free-hand, making any changes you like, or enlarge it, trace and transfer it.

Underglaze colors have a harmonic relationship with one another, like flowers in a spring garden. Be adventurous with them, and when you plan the colors to be used on your clay canvas, think in terms of color composition. If there is green on one side, maybe touches of green would balance nicely on the other. It is harmony and balance you are seeking, however, not symmetry or a mirror image.

FIG. 2-4   Organize your workspace to be most convenient and comfortable for you. I find this arrangement the best for me. Underglazes are grouped by color for quick location.

Photo by David Allison

I usually use the semi-liquid underglazes that come in little jars, and keep all of them on a tray within easy reach. The underglaze pencils I keep with my brushes. I find it best to organize the colors into color groups so as to find them easily. See Fig. 2-4.

The colors are best when they are the consistency of creamy salad dressing. Since they dry out easily, you want to keep the lids on when you are not actually using them. You can often rescue dry ones by adding a little water, so don't be too hasty about throwing them out. It is hard to bring them back to a creamy consistency, but if you dilute them and make them smooth you can use them for washes and shading.

As I mentioned before, you should think of your sketch as a guideline rather than an outline. If your sketch is a guide, your brush will follow the curves and lines of the shape you are painting, and the brushstrokes will take on their own form and dimension. One pressure stroke with a round brush can look just like a flower petal. Filling in an outline you tend not to pay attention to the smoothness, shape or direction of your brushstrokes. Because bisque is so porous and absorbent, the difference usually won't show up until you have glazed and fired your piece. See Fig. 2-5.

For most brushstrokes, you need a brush well-loaded, but not dripping, with underglaze that is not too thick. To paint a light wash or shading, as in watercolors, you will need to dilute the colors. Certain colors, such as the roses, cranberries and some yellows, will fade out in the firing if they are too diluted, so you will want to experiment and learn how the different colors behave. Making color swatches on tiles as I suggested will help you try out the colors as well as your brushstrokes.

Underglazes

I like to work out of the lid of each little underglaze container. That way I don't waste any color. Whatever is left in the lid is usable next time. Take your brush and moisten it in water. Brush lightly over a paper towel to remove excess water. If the underglaze is too dry you will need more water. Dip the brush into the container to

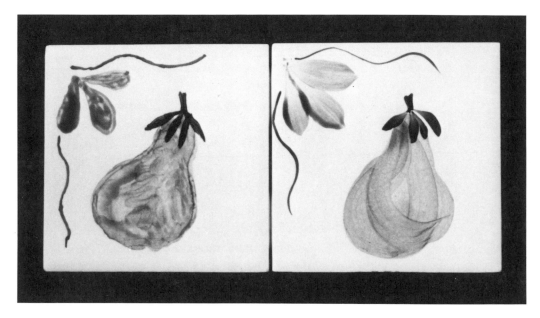

FIG. 2-5   On the tile at right, the drawing is used as a guideline for the brushstrokes. The strokes follow and reflect the shape of the object. On the tile at left, the drawing is just an outline filled with color. Not following any form or shape, the brushstrokes are uneven and messy.   *Photo by David Allison*

scoop a little color into the lid. Using your moistened brush, swoosh the color around in the lid to obtain the right consistency, turning the brush over often so that the creamy underglaze is uniformly loaded on the brush. Add water if necessary. Do a little bit at a time. That will make the consistency smoother and will help you load the brush more evenly and fully. The brush should be full but not dripping. If you are using a detail brush and the colors are too dry, use a larger brush to scoop out, dilute and blend. Then load the smaller brush.

NOTE: The colors dry quickly on the bisque, but can still smear if you touch them with your fingers, so handle the piece carefully. As much as possible, hold from the bottom. The next firing will set these colors, although you should continue to handle the pieces carefully since some smearing can still occur.

Brushes

Keep your favorite brushes in a mug or jar, with handles down and bristles up. As soon as you use a brush, rinse it in clean water. You will need to have a jar of water next to you and freshen it often. (An easy way to add a little exercise to this quiet activity!) Also have a paper towel to dry the brush on. I find it convenient to lay the three or four brushes I am using on a paper towel, next to me, so that they are easy to find and easy to reach. Don't jam brushes down into the colors, or keep the bristles down in any container. When you finish painting, wash all the brushes you used and reshape them with your fingers.

Freedom of hand movement and a well-loaded brush are the keys to smooth and flowing brushstrokes. Do not hold a brush like a pencil, with fingers close to the bristles and hand on the table. This would push the brush, causing the bristles to bend and go in different directions. Instead, hold the brush well back on the handle.

Sometimes long-handled brushes are more comfortable. If you need support, use your little finger as a prop (as a steadying force on long strokes), or rest your arm against the edge of the table. See Fig. 2-6. For some strokes you need to hold the brush in a vertical position as in Fig. 2-7; for others you need to hold it at a 45-degree angle as in Fig. 2-8. Sometimes you need to hold the handle firmly, other times you need to turn it as you make the stroke.

If painting is something new for you, practice your brushstrokes on paper with poster paints first. Then practice on bisque to understand the effects of its high absorbency. Once you are comfortable with the feel of the brushes, you won't need to practice before painting. Different brushes make different strokes. The following section is a general guide to the basic strokes you will need. Never be afraid to experiment, for there's always something new to discover.

FIG. 2-6 You will find it easier to keep your hand steady and control fine strokes if you use your little finger as support. *Photo by David Allison*

FIG. 2-7 This is how your hand will look if you are holding your brush in a vertical position. Lowering your hand a little will add the pressure you need to create a "pressure stroke." *Photo by David Allison*

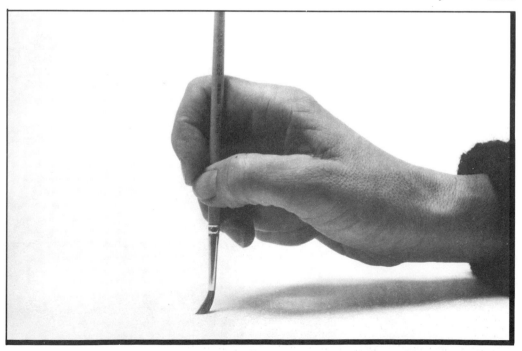

Fig. 2-8   Hold your hand at a 45-degree angle for block strokes, shading and larger area coverage.   *Photo by David Allison*

Liner Brush

To use the liner brush, shown in Fig. 2-9, hold the handle in a vertical position, letting the point touch the surface and the color flow through the brush. This will make long flowing lines, usable as flower stems, long squiggles, tendrils, etc. You can also use these brushes for writing script, but I prefer the detail brush for that. By altering the angle at which you hold the brush and by adding pressure to the stroke, you can thin or thicken the line. Held at an angle and lifting quickly, you can also make tapered strokes, narrower but similar to the pressure strokes you can make with round brushes. Use your little finger for support when you need it. Examples of these strokes are shown in Fig. 2-9.

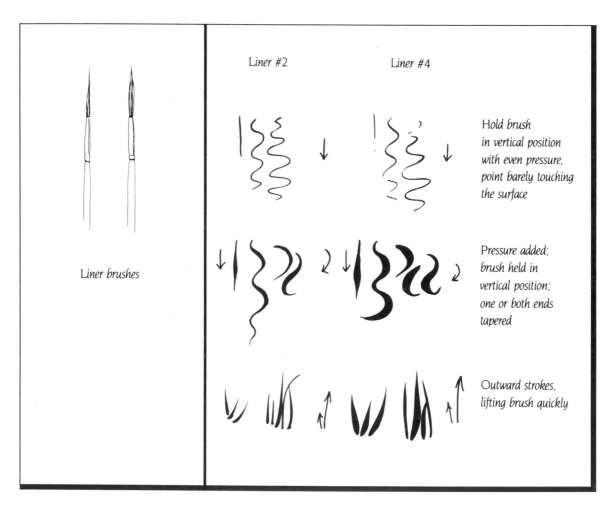

FIG. 2-9   Brushstrokes painted with a liner brush.

Round Brush

The round brush shown in Fig. 2-10, is ideal for pressure strokes. Hold the brush in a vertical position and apply additional pressure part of the time. The greater the pressure, the wider the stroke. The length of the stroke is determined by the distance traveled before swinging the brushpoint upward. Brushstrokes illustrated in Fig. 2-10 (top to bottom) are as follows: tapered at one end by starting with

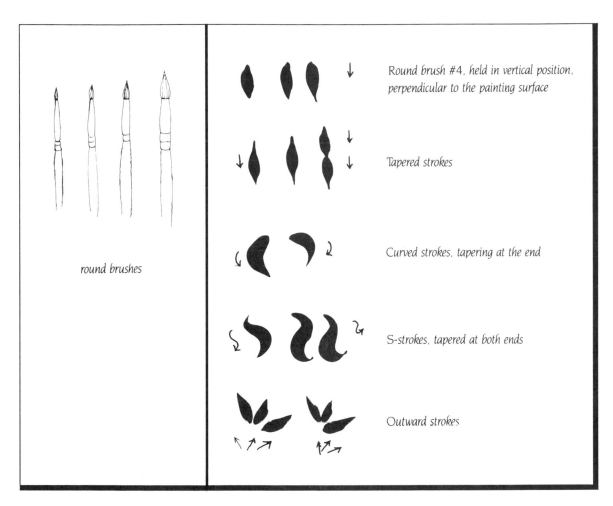

round brushes

Round brush #4, held in vertical position, perpendicular to the painting surface

Tapered strokes

Curved strokes, tapering at the end

S-strokes, tapered at both ends

Outward strokes

Fig. 2-10 Brushstrokes painted with a round brush.

pressure and ending without, or tapered at both ends by applying pressure only at the midpoint (your hand movement will determine if the stroke is straight; curved; or S-shaped). If you apply pressure evenly, and then lift the point quickly, twisting the brush as you lift, you can paint an outward stroke ideal for palm fronds, birds' tails and the like. Round brushes are also good for larger areas to be covered with three-coat underglazes. Remember to use your little finger for support.

Detail Brush

The detail brush, shown here, is basically a small, delicate round brush. Because of its fine point, it can also do some of the work of the less controllable liner brush. It is especially suited for detail work, outlining, lettering and coverage of small areas. See Fig. 2-11 and Fig. 2-12.

FIG. 2-11   Brushstrokes painted with a detail brush.

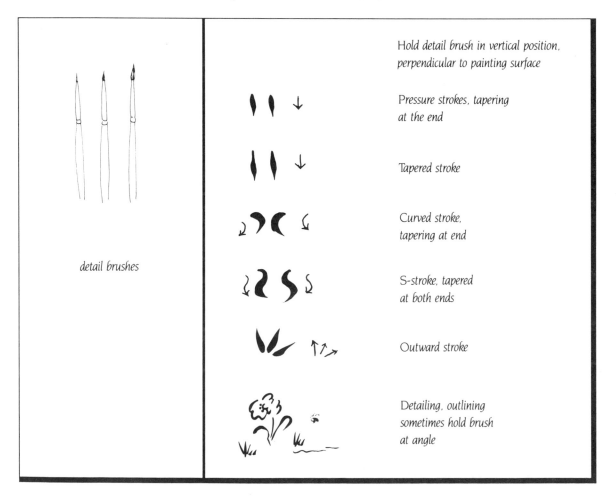

detail brushes

Hold detail brush in vertical position, perpendicular to painting surface

Pressure strokes, tapering at the end

Tapered stroke

Curved stroke, tapering at end

S-stroke, tapered at both ends

Outward stroke

Detailing, outlining sometimes hold brush at angle

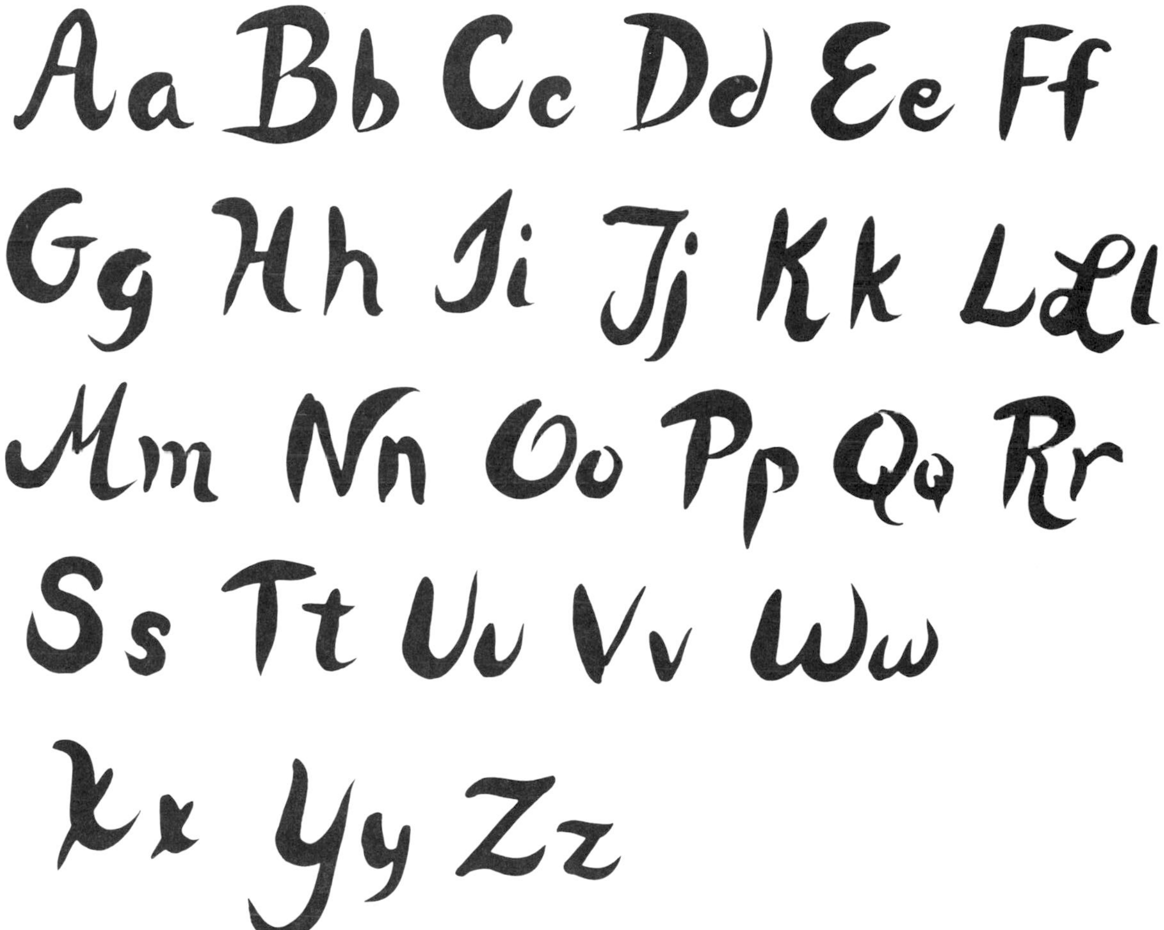

Aa Bb Cc Dd Ee Ff Gg Hh Ii Jj Kk Ll Mm Nn Oo Pp Qq Rr Ss Tt Uu Vv Ww Xx Yy Zz

Fig. 2-12 Sample alphabet painted with a detail brush.

Flat Brush

Held almost horizontally, the flat brush, shown in Fig. 2-13 (top to bottom), can be used to paint washes and do shading. Holding the brush at an angle, flat against the clay surface, you can form block strokes. These can be horizontal, vertical, long or short. Add a turn of the handle and these strokes become curves. Add arm

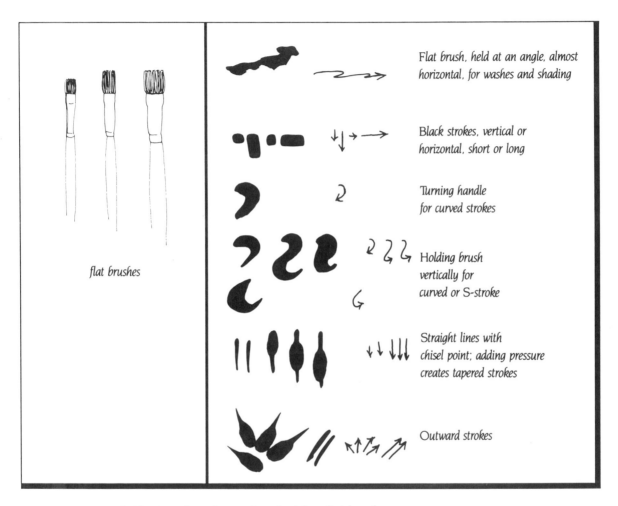

FIG. 2-13 Brushstrokes painted with a flat brush.

movement but without turning the handle, and these block strokes can become S-strokes or C-strokes. You can also hold the brush in a vertical position and take advantage of the chisel point. It can be used to paint lines or, by adding pressure, to make petal strokes. Compare these petal strokes with those you can achieve with the round brush or the fuller liner brush. The brush feels stiffer when you are using the chisel point.

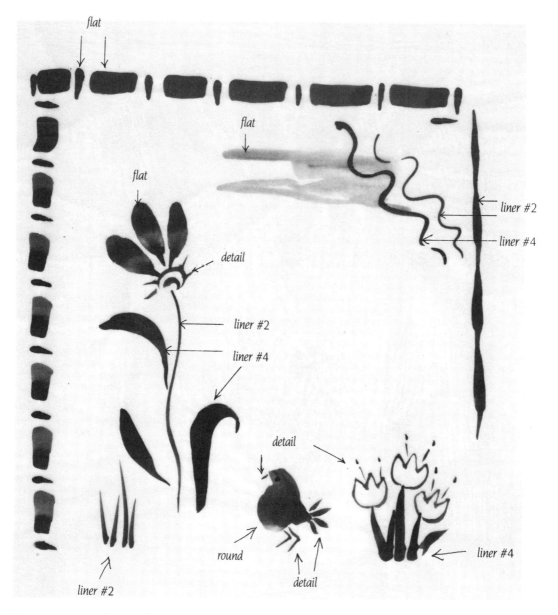

FIG. 2-14 Combining brushes and strokes to create a design.

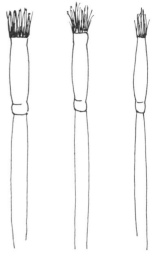

FIG. 2-15 Although you should always try to use quality brushes in good condition; raggedy, old brushes can be useful.

FIG. 2-16 Raggedy, old brushes are useful in creating uneven, bristly effects, as in leaves and palms.

Interesting and beautiful designs can be created by combining different brushes and strokes. In Fig. 2-14 the grass and flower leaves and stems were painted with liner brushes. A flat brush was used for the flower petals, clouds and border. The bird was outlined with a round brush and finished with a detailed one. Finishing touches on the flowers were also painted with a detail brush.

Another word about brushes: Although quality brushes in good condition are the ideal, ragged old brushes, as in Fig. 2-15, can be useful. These brushes can help create uneven, bristly effects, and are especially effective in painting leaves, grass, etc.

Special instructions for your practice piece: For this plate you might decide to use the following colors: royal blue for lettering and border; medium yellow for chicks and flowers; dark green for flower stems and leaves; medium green for leaves and grass; rose red for flowers; lilac for flowers; cinnamon for details on flowers and baby chicks.

Painting Your Practice Piece

1.   Load the round brush with yellow color. Use an S-shaped pressure stroke to paint the bottom half of the baby chick. Use the point to paint the top half. Remember not to dab color into the outline you have sketched. Use the outline to guide your brushstrokes. Using the same brush and making pressure strokes, paint the daisy petals on the border. Rinse the brush thoroughly.

2.   Load the round brush with rose red and paint a swirl on the border to make an easy rose. Rinse thoroughly.

3.   Load the round brush again, this time with lilac. Then with pressure strokes, make a three-petal tulip shape on the border. Rinse again.

4.   Now load the thin liner brush with dark green, and using the point, paint flowing squiggles for the longer flower stems on the border. You can use the liner or the detail brush to paint the smaller stems in the center of the plate. Rinse thoroughly. By now you probably need fresh water!

5. Load the flat brush with medium green, and making short pressure strokes, paint the leaves on the border flowers. Rinse.

6. Now it's time for the detail brush. First, load it with the royal blue, making sure it is well loaded with the creamy color. Using mild pressure strokes, do the lettering. You can also use this blue to add little dots or squiggles to the flowers, or give the baby chick blue eyes. Using appropriate colors, add all the little details— baby chick's feet, little flowers in the grass. (Don't forget to rinse between colors.) Don't worry if it doesn't look realistic. Think about color and pattern and rhythm. Does that area need a touch of blue? Or yellow? Or red? Does it look balanced? Cheerful? Does it have charm? Remember, this is a baby plate.

7. Use your detail brush to sign or write a message on the back. Blue is my favorite color for lettering. Brown, black and green also work, but red and yellow don't do well at all. Remember to handle the plate carefully so that you don't smear your painting.

Congratulations. The creative part has been completed! (Or should I say the worst is over?) Now it's on to the finishing tasks.

Second Firing: Setting the Colors

This process is much like the first firing, since we are still at the bisque stage. You will again fire to cone 04, but since there is almost no moisture in the clay you can fire faster: one hour at low, one at medium and then to high until done. Again, let cool twice as long as it took to fire.

> Special instructions for your practice piece: Fire to cone 04. All pencil marks will disappear, and you will see what your creation basically will look like. Color changes in the underglazes won't show up at this stage. If you want to add anything, color or detail, this is your last chance. If it's just a little detail you do not need to refire.

Glazing

This is not difficult. The most important thing to remember is that everything should be dust-free—the piece, the brush and the bowl in which you are putting the glaze.

1.   Brush off the piece with a duster brush, still being careful not to smear the painting with your fingers.

2.   Put down clean newspaper to protect your table from the glaze.

3.   Pour some food-safe, clear, gloss glaze into a bowl (a clean margarine tub is perfect). Only pour in what you need for you can always add. Normally the glaze is the right consistency (like slightly thin yogurt), but if it is really thick you can add a few drops of water, making sure to blend it in completely.

4.   Using your glaze brush, cover all parts of the piece with one generous smooth coat of glaze. Be careful not to have it so thickly applied that it drips, for that will show on the finished piece. I find that longer strokes are better than dabs. Let this coat dry completely (it gets lighter in color as it dries). Apply a second coat. Some glazes require three coats, so be sure to read the label. The glaze will cover your painting, but don't panic! This opaque coat will, in the firing, turn into a clear, glossy surface over your painting, protecting it and making it shine.

Potters often use their index finger, covered with glaze, to add or touch up glaze on areas that didn't get enough (where your fingers were holding the piece while you glazed, for instance). This can smear the underglaze painting underneath, so try to use a brush instead, unless it's a place where there is no decoration.

Hints for Glazing:

* ✳   Turn pieces over and do the bottoms first, so that the top sides and edges will be sure to remain smooth.

* ✳   When doing containers such as mugs, vases and pitchers, do the bottoms first. Then take some of the glaze, thin it slightly with water and blend to buttermilk consistency. Pour it into the container, and roll it around until the inside surface is completely covered. Then pour out the excess. (You can pour it back into the margarine tub.) A second coat is usually not required with this method.

* ✳   Apply one coat on the outside of the container and let dry; apply a second coat and let dry.

* ✳   Do handles last—and don't forget to coat the undersides.

NOTE: Low-fire ceramics need to be completely glazed, even the bottoms. The bisque is not vitrified, i.e., there is still some porosity. If areas are left unglazed, moisture can still enter the piece and sometimes discolor the design with time. For this reason, I also suggest not using low-fire ceramics to bake in, although they can withstand the heat.

> **Special instructions for your practice piece:** Following the glazing procedure described in the preceding section, glaze your plate, first the back (both coats), then the front. Let the glaze brush follow the curve of the plate. On the back of the plate, apply glaze in broad, half-circle strokes, working from the outside in toward the center. Repeat on the front of the plate. Don't overload the brush so as to create drips. Reload the brush as needed, not letting the brush get too dry. (NOTE: A dry brush can rub off some of the glaze already applied.)

Third Firing: Glaze Firing

1. Vacuum out the kiln, if necessary, and once in a while just in case. Vacuum inside and on the top edge, so as to prevent dust settling on the glaze.

2. Now you can load the kiln, making sure that every piece is placed on a stilt, so that the glaze does not touch and then stick to the bottom of the kiln. Make sure that no glazed pieces touch each other, including lids and containers. This will prevent them from sticking together. When loading the kiln, try to plan it so that the heat will distribute evenly. The bottom of the kiln is the coolest, so I like to place vertical, rather than flat pieces there.

3. Place an 06 (lower temperature than before) cone on the kiln sitter, then set the automatic timer.

4. Keeping peepholes open, and with proper ventilation, you can now turn on the kiln. Fire one hour on low, one on medium and then on high until finished.

5. Let kiln cool completely. This is vital for this firing, because the glaze as well as the piece can suffer thermal shock and crack if cooled too suddenly. Even if the piece itself doesn't crack, the glaze can. This is called crazing, and makes the glaze not completely food-safe anymore.

6.   After taking your plate out of the kiln, rub the stilt marks off the bottom of the plate with the stilt stone.

> **Special instructions for your practice piece:** Following the procedures described in the preceding section, place your plate on a stilt in a dust-free kiln, and fire to cone 06. Cool completely, and then remove stilt marks.

Preventing and Correcting Firing Problems

Firing can be complicated if you are dealing with a variety of clays, glazes and techniques. Since you will basically always have the same firing conditions, you should encounter very few problems. Some problems can be corrected, while some cannot. Most are preventable, however, so I would like to explain them and give you the means and background to avoid them.

Several of the following problems are a result of under- or over-firing. If this occurs, check your equipment. Did you use the correct cone? Did the cone work and trigger the kiln sitter? Did the kiln shut off sooner or later than you anticipated? Is the switch working? Are the heating elements working?

Crazing

Crazing is an uneven network of fine hairline cracks that appears in the glazed surface of a finished ceramic piece. (NOTE: Some crazing, evenly distributed, is intentional, and done with special glazes.) This is the most common problem encountered. It is usually caused by under-fired bisque, cooling the kiln too quickly, thermal shock to the piece or incompatibility of the glaze to the clay body. Crazing can occur immediately or happen later. You can sometimes hear the ping when it happens. Under-fired (also known as immature) bisque means the greenware was not fired hot or long enough. Consequently, the glaze does not "fit" properly and cracks. In delayed crazing, it is usually because the immature bisque has absorbed moisture, swollen and cracked the glaze. Crazing is not always unattractive, but it does mean that the surface is no longer completely food-safe.

Prevention: Make sure to fire greenware properly. Don't "shock" the piece with extreme changes in temperature. Also check kiln.

Correction: Refire the piece to cone 05, or even cone 04, to mature the bisque, and refire the glaze.

NOTE: Repeated dishwasher use will sometimes craze dishes.

Craters and Bubbles

Cratered or bubbled glaze is usually caused by under-firing the bisque, or applying glaze too thickly.

Prevention: Glaze and fire properly as directed. Also check your equipment.

Correction: This problem is hard to correct, but sometimes you can grind down the blemishes with a stilt stone, lightly reglaze and then refire to cone 05 or 04.

Pinholes

Pinhole glaze is usually caused by under-fired bisque, dust on the bisque or in the kiln, applying glaze to greenware instead of bisque, or firing too rapidly.

Prevention: Be neat, be patient and follow directions.

Correction: Fill in just the holes with very thick glaze and refire to cone 05. Or put a thin coat over the whole surface and refire to cone 05.

Crawling

Crawled glaze occurs when the glaze pulls (crawls) away from the surface, leaving bare spots. This problem is often caused by too heavy an application of underglaze (the three-coat kind), oil from the skin or accumulation of dust on the bisque (in the bottom of a pitcher, for instance). Hard spots can be caused by over-sponging greenware, which creates sealed or polished areas that don't absorb the glaze. Crawling can also be caused by putting greenware too close to the heating element, thereby burning it and making it less absorbent.

Fill a pitcher with fresh flowers and start your day with a cheerful breakfast setting. Handpainted ceramics combine easily with plain white china. *Photo by David Allison*

Delightful styles of handpainted ceramics; pieces include a lovely old Dutch Delft vase, a small French faience bowl, a fine Portuguese pitcher, a Greek plate and several colorful Italian ceramics. *Photo by David Allison*

A personalized wedding pitcher makes a lovely gift. (See Commemorative Project #2 in Chapter 6.) *Photo by David Allison*

Assortment of brushes and paints used to create a pleasing plate design.

Handpainted dishes and accessories make you feel at home. The fruit bowl is the same one seen elsewhere in the color section.

Photo by David Allison

This lamp base is an example of an item you can design and paint to fit into a chosen setting, coordinating it to other accessories or a favorite fabric. (See "Decorative Project #4," in Chapter 6.)

Photo by David Allison

Large pasta bowl (16″ diameter) with a Venetian theme. Not visible is the floral design on the outside.
Photo by Donna Cantor

Deep bowl (10″ diameter) with a scene based on a photograph, and a border of colorful birds. The outside of this bowl can be seen in the place setting shown in this color section. *Photo by Donna Cantor*

Tile scenes or motifs set into tables make practical and charming pieces to be used indoors or out. Tables can be made of metal or wood.

Photos by Donna Cantor

This small room is the heart of our house. Every wall is filled with color and design, and things lovingly made and joyfully collected. Signor Deo's tile scenes keep company with clay canvases painted in Italy, France, Portugal and our own Virginia home.

Photos by David Allison

A few handpainted tiles and a vase, painted to coordinate with the shower curtain, add a handcrafted and custom look to an otherwise ordinary bathroom. *Photo by David Allison*

When we added onto our house we had to give up the bathroom window. This small tile mural of the view from our balcony in Naples replaced the window. *Photo by David Allison*

Prevention: Clean greenware before it "ages" to avoid having to over-clean. Dust thoroughly, making sure not to forget the inside of containers. Place correctly in the kiln.

Correction: Sometimes reglazing and firing will help.

Cloudiness and Discoloring

Cloudy glaze is often due to glaze being too heavy or being under-fired.

Prevention: Be more sparing with how much glaze you put on. Also check kiln.

Correction: Refire to one cone higher (cone 05).

Grayed or discolored glaze is usually caused by over-firing, the piece being too close to the heating element or insufficient ventilation.

Prevention: Fire properly.

Correction: This problem is hard to correct, but you can try reglazing and firing to the proper cone.

Graininess

Grainy glaze means you put the glaze on too thin (and just when you thought you got it right).

Prevention: Glaze with sufficient but not overabundant coats. Like paint or varnish on wood, glaze will drip if too thick, but will seem grainy, if the coat is too thin.

Correction: This problem is easy to correct. Heat the piece slightly in your home oven. Then apply a full, even coat of glaze. (Heating the plate helps the glaze adhere.) Refire to cone 06.

Adding Gold or Silver

Gold or silver are added on top of the finished glaze, and therefore, are not food-safe. I use them rarely for that reason, but they can add a touch of formality and elegance to a piece, and also give you the opportunity to add a custom detail, such as a name or date, to an already finished piece. I find the easiest way to add gold or silver is to use a pen made specially for that purpose. It works like a fine pointed felt-tip pen.

1. To start, remove cap and depress the top on a scrap of paper. Hold until the gold or silver appears on the tip.

2. Write slowly and evenly to allow for an adequate flow of color. Hold more vertically than you would a regular pen. Because of the thin line made, you can outline or write easily.

3. Fire to cone 018, allowing for sufficient ventilation.

Summary

From beginning to end, this is what needs to happen if a blob of clay is to become a finished, handpainted work of art.

1. Make the piece to be painted using hand-formed, thrown or slipcast methods.

2. Get the piece ready for painting by cleaning the greenware and firing to hard bisque (cone 04).

3. Paint the design after sketching it, and fire the piece to cone 04 to set colors.

4. Coat the piece completely with glaze and fire to cone 06. Then remove stilt marks.

3

General Safety Precautions

*T*his chapter is not so interesting to read, but is important to know. Common sense will help your five senses guide you to safety, but I've outlined some general rules as reminders.

Be Clean and Neat

The less dust on you, and especially in you, the better.

- ❖ Make sure your work area is well ventilated.

- ❖ Keep work and storage areas free of dust, cleaning with a wet mop or sponge.

- ❖ Clean up spills immediately.

- ❖ Clean glaze jar rims before closing, so that dried glaze doesn't build up and then crumble off.

- ❖ Wash brushes immediately after use.

Be Sensible

❖ Don't eat, drink or inhale ceramic products.

❖ Be careful not to combine ceramic products with food or drink.

❖ Protect cuts or open wounds from foreign material.

❖ Wash hands and arms thoroughly after working.

❖ Don't use containers or utensils for ceramics that will later be used in the kitchen.

Use Protective Equipment

❖ Use apron or smock to protect clothing from dust and glazes. Wear mask if you are susceptible to allergies or find the dust bothers you.

❖ Don't wear contact lenses where the environment is too dusty.

❖ Use kiln gloves to handle hot kiln or take out still hot ceramics. (Not too hot, of course. Remember that opening the kiln too early can cause breakage!)

❖ Use a stilt stone to smooth down stilt marks on glazed and fired pieces. Those marks can be very sharp.

❖ Additional equipment will be required if you decide to use a sprayer for glazing or an airbrush for painting.

Know the Products You Are Using

Read the labels to know what underglazes, glazes and overglazes you are using, and follow application and firing instructions. Remember to read labels when you are changing product brands. Don't assume that similar products by different manufacturers have the same ingredients.

❖ Underglazes—most underglazes are considered food-safe when a food-safe glaze is used over them.

❖ Glazes—our main concern for this book is whether the glaze is food-safe, that is, whether lead- and cadmium-release levels are low enough. Labels are clearly marked.

❖ Overglazes—should not be used on surfaces that will be used for food or drink. Use only for decorative purposes.

Follow manufacturers' directions for safe use of equipment and kilns.

❖ Have kiln properly installed, meeting all local electrical codes.

❖ Make sure to provide proper ventilation for the kiln. This may include installation of an exhaust fan or air-handling system. If something has a strong smell, you probably should not be inhaling it.

❖ Wear dark-shaded glasses from a safety-supply house for looking into peep-holes.

❖ Use kiln gloves to handle hot kiln and fired ceramics.

❖ Don't operate kiln in a wet area.

❖ Keep children away from kiln.

❖ Don't open kiln while it is firing. Wait until it has shut off and cooled down.

❖ Don't leave paper or other combustibles near a firing kiln.

Reevaluate Your Safety Needs

Reevaluate your safety needs if you add major equipment or start doing things you never did before. Ask questions, read all the literature, and when in doubt, talk to a professional. For instance, if you start pouring your own molds, mixing clays, or using spray or airbrush equipment, you will have to be even more concerned about proper ventilation.

4

"What Should I Make? What Will My Canvas Be?"

*T*he first question to answer is whether you are making this ceramic piece for yourself or for someone else. It is easy to please nearly everyone when you give handpainted ceramics as gifts. There are innumerable ways to personalize your gifts for those close to you or for special occasions. The color section and the next chapter will give you many ideas. Handpainted ceramics are decorative, functional, elegant and friendly all at once—great gifts for close friends or new acquaintances.

The piece you decide on can be casual (a mug) or formal (a vase), for special occasions (a wedding pitcher, a Passover plate) or for everyday use (dishes, a door plaque, a lamp). The list is endless.

Most of what you will make will be relatively small and transportable, but with this versatile skill you are about to develop, you will be able to undertake larger projects such as handpainted tile backsplashes, countertops in your kitchen, or beautiful, tiled fireplace surrounds in your living room. Tiles have endless uses indoors and out. You will be amazed what you, with just a few materials, can accomplish.

FIG. 4-1 "Dancing the Continental," one of the first ceramic pieces I painted.

59

"What Should I Make? What will my Canvas Be?"

Fig. 4-2 Tiles are wonderful little canvases, each telling their own story. These 4" × 4" paintings can be set into walls, becoming part of a greater whole, or they can just be used casually as coasters or spoon rests.

As I mentioned earlier, ceramic shops have a wide variety of greenware to choose from. But don't limit yourself to only what is on their shelves for most shops only pour the most commonly sold molds. If you have something in mind, don't hesitate to ask. Shops have many catalogues to show you, and many molds in their pouring rooms. If there is something unique you are interested in and cannot find it in any shop or catalog, don't despair. Talk to your local potter (or pottery student). Potters will often make, or throw, pieces to order and will have access to the clay you need. Just remember to explain that you want to paint on low-fire clay. In case your mind goes blank and you just need a reminder of what you can paint on, here are some possibilities:

"WHAT SHOULD I MAKE? WHAT WILL MY CANVAS BE?"

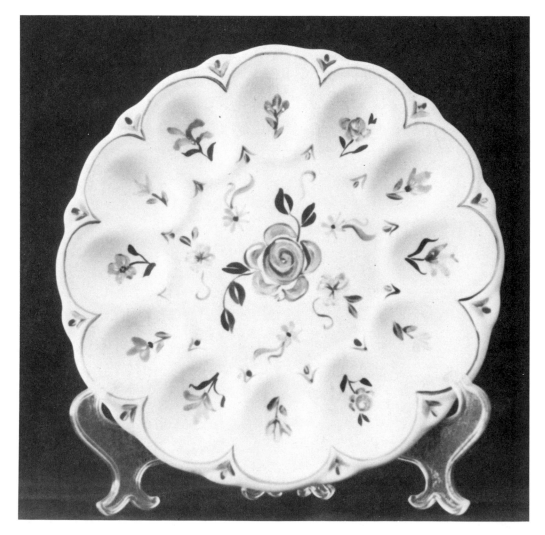

FIG. 4-3 A delicate egg plate makes a lovely addition to anyone's china. For variation, a small scene can be painted on the center space.

FIG. 4-4 Ceramic baskets can be used all around the house. Many shapes and sizes are available. Just like straw baskets, they can be used to hold anything from letters to dinner rolls.

FIG. 4-5 This mantle clock was decorated with a floral design and made into a commemorative piece with the addition of the date. A name in the lower panel could further personalize this piece. Clockworks are easy to obtain and attach.

63

"What Should I Make? What will my Canvas Be?"

FIG. 4-6 Personalized—and dated—Christmas ornaments are another opportunity to create miniature paintings. You can make them annual gifts so that people will look forward to them.

❋ Individual tiles—for trivets, coasters, spoon rests or just as miniature paintings.

❋ Groups of tiles—to be used as backsplashes, countertops, fireplace surrounds, tabletops, trays, large trivets, message boards or pictures to be framed. Put them on window sills or set them into walls, inside or outside.

You can frame your doors and windows with them, or use them as base-boards or on stair risers. (NOTE: Low-fire clay tiles are not well suited for floors.)

✳ Tableware—plates, bowls, cups, mugs, platters, teapots, coffee pots, pitchers, egg plates, sugar and creamer, salt and pepper.

✳ Accessories—candlesticks, sconces, watering cans, planters, vases, baskets, lamp bases and clock faces. (Wiring and clock works are usually available from your ceramic shop also.)

✳ Boxes, canisters, or other things with lids.

✳ House-shaped boxes and canisters with smooth walls to paint scenes on.

✳ Smooth-surfaced Christmas ornaments.

✳ Door plaques and other signs.

✳ Bathroom accessories.

. . . and so forth.

Remember, paint what you enjoy. I like painting on things that someone will really use. Although it is nice to hang ceramics on the wall, it's even nicer to be able to comfortably handle your work. Don't be afraid of it. Low-fire ceramics chip more easily than porcelain, but glazed properly, they are food-safe, dishwasher-safe and certainly heat- and waterproof.

5

"How Do I Develop My Own Designs?"

*A*fter you have chosen the piece you want to work on you'll have to decide how to decorate it. But the question "What should I paint?" will only be difficult to answer the first few times you ask. The possibilities are unlimited, and the question "What should I paint?" will soon be replaced by "What should I paint *first*?"

Later in this chapter are many suggestions for subjects and themes for your work; and the next chapter describes several specific design projects. But your real goal is to learn how to develop your own ideas and your own look.

Developing "original" designs is not as overwhelming an undertaking as it may sound. If you explore the works of other artists and designers, you will learn to see through new eyes and consequently you will develop the ability to absorb, interpret and redefine what you see. With this ability, you will find inspiration all around you. You will find that different arts have different things to teach. Illustrators, for instance, are especially gifted at distilling the essentials from what they see or want to see. Fabric designers are strong in the use of color and pattern. Both of these skills can be applied to ceramic painting. The more forms of art, craft and design you are familiar with, the greater your sources of inspiration. Every imaginative use of color, line, form or composition that you become familiar with will increase the vocabulary with which you can express yourself.

Looking at Designs

Learning to see is as important as learning to paint. It means learning how to explore a design or pattern. Have you ever noticed that when television programs cover art exhibits you are not just shown one photograph of a painting? Instead the camera travels over the painting, showing different sections of it as if they were parts of a landscape too large for the eye to take in all at once. Details of a painting take on individual importance and became independent works of art. It is a wonderful discovery, for it means finding a myriad of designs within the one larger design.

You can make your own traveling camera with just two pieces of paper. Cut each into L-shaped pieces, 1" to 2" wide. Each leg of the "L" should be at least 5" long. Placing them with the corners diagonally opposite each other you will have an adjustable frame. With this opening travel over the design. When you look at designs in this way, paper frame in hand, you will find it much easier to think about the many possibilities a design offers. See Fig. 5-1. You can rearrange the whole design or just part of it, turn it upside down, simplify it, elaborate it, change the composition, add to it or subtract from it. Take part of it and make it larger or repeat it. Take all of it, reduce it and add a different border.

When you are trying to coordinate a ceramic piece to a fabric or wallpaper, this tool will give you many ideas to choose from. Don't be afraid to combine ideas. A detail from one source, may be just the thing to put with a detail from another. That is what will make your designs original. You will soon find your own point of view, and you will recognize it, for it will be comfortable for you.

Compiling Your Idea Library

Your "idea library" is to be a collection of images to which you can refer again and again. See Fig. 5-2. You will find it not only helpful but also wonderful fun to put together. Use these references often: try them out; reinterpret them; mix them

Fig. 5-1   Use an adjustable paper frame to pick out details you find interesting. Details seen in isolation often have a different feeling than the design or picture as a whole.

Photo by David Allison

up, combining elements of one with elements of another. As you do this you will extract those things that are essential to your point of view, and you will develop your own style. I have offered some suggestions to start you off. The "Resources" section provides more specific information and additional suggestions.

Books

Books provide an unlimited source of inspiration. Since you will never run out of books to look at, the question is where to start.

FIG. 5-2 There are wonderful design ideas everywhere. If you gather them together and organize them you will build an invaluable idea library to be used and referred to again and again.   *Photo by David Allison*

Start, of course, by looking at what other ceramists and potters have done over the centuries. There are innumerable histories of pottery, ceramics and porcelain. You will find many things to inspire you, and you will be able to try out many of the things you see by using the techniques described in this book.

Decorating with Tiles is a lavishly illustrated book that will make you want to tile everything around you! But don't forget that all those designs can be adapted to three-dimensional pieces also.

Dover Books is a wonderful publisher, offering a wide variety of inexpensive design reference books filled with great ideas in styles that will meet almost anyone's requirements.

Art books about painting, illustration, graphic, advertising and fashion design are brimming with ideas. Explore different styles and periods: art deco, art nouveau, Egyptian, American Indian, Dutch or Abstract Expressionism.

It is hard to have clear pictures in your mind of everything you might want to paint, so I have found it very useful to use such reference materials as field guides for trees, animals, sea shells, flowers and birds.

Illustrators of children's books have the ability to simplify and clarify shapes, proportions and details, and there are many wonderful styles and books to choose from. Because children's illustrations are often as decorative as they are descriptive, you will find much to inspire you.

Naive art, especially European, is a wonderful resource for ceramists. The style and mood suit the everydayness of ceramics especially well.

Carl Larsson's Home (Reading, MA: Addison-Wesley Publishing Company, 1981) is a book about the home of the Swedish artist. It will inspire you to think of everything around you as worthy of art—your art.

And then last, but certainly not least, I would like to recommend the book *The Art of Zandra Rhodes* (Boston, MA: Houghton Mifflin Company, 1985). It is a wonderful study of the creative process, and a first-hand view of how one very gifted artist and designer interprets images and translates them into original designs that express her own unique point of view.

Magazines

Decorating, craft, art and antiques magazines of all kinds will be of interest to you. Your local library should have many for you to look at. If any magazines particularly appeal to you, you may want to get a subscription. Also craft supply stores often have a wide variety of craft magazines, and you may want to look through tole painting, decorative painting, embroidery, needlepoint and quilting magazines. Since you may not have space to keep all these magazines, cut out those things that interest you and file them or put them in an album.

Children's Drawings

Children have the ability to find interest in the simplest objects, and will create a full design out of just a few objects. It seems to be a natural talent that somewhere along the line adults forget that they have. (See color section for examples of children's work.)

Catalogues

Tile, china and porcelain catalogues are the most obvious. But mail-order and auction catalogues are also a wonderful compendium of beautifully designed cards, scarves, porcelains and so forth. Cut out the best pictures and put them in your file.

Other Sources

One terrific source is other people's ceramics! Another one is paper table-ware, which often has lovely designs and translates well to the techniques you are learning here.

Fabric and textile designs are displayed in books. You can look at these or you can simply look at swatch books. I personally find chintzes wonderful for learning how to balance colors and create compact, dense designs. But your versions can be simpler. Use only certain details, omitting others; change colors or leave some out; or use another background color. In fact, experimentation is how you learn to coordinate ceramics and fabrics.

Wallpaper designs are another good source. Again, look through sample books.

Greeting cards, note cards, postcards, posters, giftwrap, giftbags and adver-tisements also offer interesting designs.

Stay alert, ideas lurk everywhere! You will find good design in unexpected places. If you can't put the object in your library, take a picture or make a sketch of it.

Organizing Your Idea Library

As your collection gets bigger, you can organize it in ways most useful to you. You'll want to be able to enjoy re-looking at all the manifestations of art and design that you have found. Books and magazines are easy to organize, but what about all those individual pieces of paper or fabric? You can put them in photo albums and create your own art books. Or use a file box, dividing the ideas into categories: people, animals, landscapes, flowers, fruit, vegetables, borders, holidays, etc. Cross reference the ideas if it helps. To this file you can also add the sketches that you are making. (NOTE: If all the separate pieces of paper are the same size they will be much easier to file. You can use inexpensive construction paper as the backing for smaller pieces.)

Don't forget to take pictures of your own work too, so that you can remember all your own ideas. You'll find it interesting to see how your own style changes and develops. A shoe box with 4" × 6" index cards as dividers makes an easy file for photographs. Date the photographs and then file them by category. In this way you can look up how you did something in the past.

If you decide to start your ceramic painting career by trying out some of the projects in Chapter 6, remember to make them your own. Add or subtract design elements; simplify or substitute; combine ideas from one project with ideas from another. In Chapter 4 we talked about choosing the canvas—that is, choosing the object on which to paint. Don't forget that, except for tiles, ceramics are three-dimensional. You can paint on the outside, inside, underneath and all around—or just on a part. The first gift I made was a mug for an old friend with whom I had spent hours watching Fred Astaire movies. On the outside I painted Fred and Ginger dancing and my friend's name on the marquee. On the inside I painted a stick-figure chorus line kicking their heels. I covered every inch!

Having chosen the article, your first decision will be whether the design is to be commemorative or purely decorative.

Commemorative Designs

Commemorative designs are obviously meant to commemorate a time, an event, a place or a person—or all of them at once. The better you know someone the easier this will be. Your friends and family will be quite delighted at seeing moments of their life commemorated in your work. But let me be more specific and give you some ideas to use or build on. Don't hesitate to use photographs as references. You don't have to be completely accurate. If you are doing people, you will find that if the hair color is right, and the person is more or less, in relation to other things, the right size, everyone will think you have done a perfect portrait. It is what you choose to depict that will touch people's hearts, not the accuracy of the depiction.

Family Tree

There are many ways to create a family tree. The one that comes immediately to mind, of course, is the standard tree, with the grandparents' names at the top, and working down to the current generation. Another nice way, however, is shown in Fig. 5-3. The ancestors are painted as little portraits in the tree, and the current, living family is shown standing at the foot of the tree. That makes it possible to show both sides of the family. A family tree works well on a platter or on a vertical piece such as a vase or pitcher. This is a wonderful present for grandparents, who will love seeing their pasts and their futures depicted. And if the hair colors are right your relatives will recognize themselves immediately!

Birth of a Baby

A wonderful way to commemorate the birth of a baby is to make something that the parents will love to look at and that the baby could actually use one day. My most popular orders are baby plates. You can add bowls and mugs to this. Tile scenes are also lovely. Create a colorful scene with children's themes and you will delight parents and child. Incorporate the child's name and birthdate, and perhaps other facts such as height, weight and place of birth. You can also incorporate

Fig. 5-3 This family tree shows the current generation at the foot of the tree and past generations in the branches. It is one of many ways a family tree can be depicted.
Photo by David Allison

details from the family such as older siblings, the fact that they have a beautiful garden or an old family dog, or that the mother is a lawyer and the father quilts. If you can't draw people, draw teddy bears, ducks, cats, or even cartoons or stick figures. A sample design for you to try is in Chapter 6.

Birthday

Everyone gets older, and aging is no reason to stop celebrating. You can commemorate birthdays by painting places, people and events in scenes or just incorporating the name and date in a colorful floral design. If you start with a birth gift, think of using a piece you can add to on subsequent birthdays. Dishes are nice for that. One of my customers orders annual plates for her children, incorporating their current interests, favorite activities and even nicknames.

Wedding

Here's another one of those grand events! Weddings are fun, and so are the scenes you can paint. You can show the place the couple got married (use photographs), or show the whole family gathered in a garden, under a tree or feasting on wedding cake. You might even add some musicians—and don't forget to include the happy couple's names and wedding date.

If you don't know the couple at all, you can simply set their names and wedding date into a floral design. Pitchers seem appropriate objects to paint on for this occasion, as do platters. I had an imaginative customer who asked for a wedding platter with the state birds and state flowers of both the bride and groom. Many of your ideas will be appropriate for anniversaries as well as weddings. A personalized wedding pitcher design is shown in Chapter 6.

Favorite Places or House Portraits

House portraits have long been popular. People always have other places they have loved too—places they have lived or gone to on vacation. Refer to photographs and incorporate little details, if you can, that make those places unique to them. An example of a house portrait done on tiles is shown in Chapter 6.

The largest commemorative work I have done is a 17-foot kitchen backsplash. The scene included the family, their pets, their house, their favorite vacation place, the pond where Grandpa takes their son fishing, and so forth. Try to think like Grandma Moses.

Favorite places can be imaginary too. You can create a mood by painting a scene. A spring garden or a clearing in the forest are just right in a country-style room; a stylish art-deco theme may be the perfect thing to place on the grand piano. See color section for examples.

Favorite Animals

Try pet portraits or scenes with favorite animals in them. You know how it is: some people love anteaters and can't find anything with anteaters on them. Anthropomorphic animals can also be used any number of ways and are fun. Use them to take the place of people. Beatrix Potter and Richard Scarry are masters at this, and their children's books will inspire you.

And don't forget dog and cat bowls—their owners will be delighted.

Holidays and Religious Occasions

Christmas, Passover, Hanukkah, Easter, Christening, Communion, Confirmation, Bar Mitzvah and Thanksgiving are reasons for commemorating. You can use symbols or paint scenes. Again, see color section for examples.

Other Special Events

Graduations, retirement and achievements will be remembered with special pride if the important person receives one of your commemorative pieces.

"Thanks"

Personalized ceramics are wonderful, thoughtful thank you gifts for teachers, scout leaders, coaches, school bus drivers, nurses and people who have shown you kindnesses. Include names, dates, places and relevant details such as team members' names, depiction of a soccer player, girl scout, a crossing guard or classroom scene.

Special Interests

Paint something you love, or that the special person in your life loves. This can be anything: Fred Astaire, football, quilting, pelicans, violins or orchids.

In this section I have just listed some of the possibilities. You will think of many more. Remember there are no rules and no limitations.

Decorative Designs

Decorative designs are meant to be exactly that. Their primary objective is to beautify their surroundings. And since you are the creator of these designs, you have the golden opportunity of personalizing these designs. Personalization can be commemorative, in the ways I described in the preceding section, or it can be a style that reflects your personality. There are many ways that this can, and quite naturally, will happen. Just by the fact that you are the designer and the painter, your work will be unique to you. Even on simple, standard floral designs, your colors and brushstrokes will reflect you. It will be your touch that is felt, and your interpretation of that design that is expressed.

You can customize your designs in more specific ways too. You can design your ceramics to coordinate with fabrics, echoing the patterns or the colors, or taking details from the fabric and incorporating them in your ceramic design.

I produced two such designs for a client. One client wanted her kitchen backsplash tiles to match her wallpaper. Because of the colors and scale of her wallpaper pattern, I was able to duplicate it quite faithfully.

She had something very different in mind for the tiles around her fireplace. She asked for designs that would reflect her family's interest in the sea. But she also wanted them to coordinate with the blue chintz fabric in her living room. To achieve this I painted the individual tiles with things from the sea (their boat, fish, a fisherman, etc.) and tied them together with a blue-based border that echoed the colors in the fabric.

You can practice coordinating fabric and ceramics by trying the lamp base project in Chapter 6.

You can design dishes to go with tiles or tiles to go with dishes. Or design your own serving pieces for dishes you already have by matching colors or patterns, or creating new designs that coordinate and tie the two together.

As you become experienced and practiced at developing your own original designs, you will be able to adapt that ability to other media—painting on other surfaces, designing needlework, etc.—and think in terms of multi-media projects. Some ideas along these lines are:

- Ceramics designed and handpainted to coordinate with or complement your embroidery, appliqué, quilting, needlepoint or fabric painting.

- Ceramics (especially tiles) designed and handpainted to coordinate with or complement your stencilled or handpainted furniture, walls or window and door trim.

$$6$$

Design Projects

*I*n this chapter I have put together some design projects for you to try. You will find that they cover many of the ideas we discussed in the preceding chapters. You'll have the chance to try some commemorative themes as well as some decorative ones. You'll experiment with a variety of styles: floral, abstract, a scene and a children's theme. And you will paint on an assortment of shapes. Following the "General Instructions," I have provided specific information for each project.

Choose a project and pick out an appropriate piece of greenware. Remember to keep it simple. Then fire or have it fired to bisque. Use commercially manufactured and bisque-fired tiles, if possible.

Now you are ready to paint. Drawings for each project are provided for guidance. Looking at the drawing, use a regular pencil to draw your own version on the bisque. Most of you won't find this difficult at all, but I know that some of you will feel intimidated by the thought of drawing free-hand. Don't panic and run to get your tracing paper! Remember, you've already done the Practice Piece in Chapter 2. Besides, pencil is erasable so there's no harm done if you have to try a few times. You can practice on paper first, but it's just as easy on bisque. And don't worry about smudges—they fire out. Flat pieces are a bit easier to draw on, so you might want to start with one of them. Don't hesitate to change my drawing, for this is your work. With a little practice you will gain confidence drawing free-hand, and you will find it natural to substitute, add, subtract or combine—in short, to add your own touches and ideas. (If you would like to trace and transfer a drawing to your piece, please see Chapter 2 for instructions.) Finished pieces are shown in the color section.

Next to subject, colors are the most personal decision. I find dark blue the best for lettering, but other colors work too. Only reds and yellows are not good candidates, for they have a tendency to fade out.

Have fun! And don't forget to sign your work—all those future generations will want to know your name.

Commemorative Project #1: Baby Plate

Here you will get a chance to think like a child. The design is relatively simple, but there's room for more details. Perhaps you would like to add more animals, birds, flowers or toys to the center or the border? The child's name can be incorporated into the design itself—on a wagon or balloon? Perhaps you'd like some reference to the family: a sibling, a special place or a family pet. I like just the name and birthdate on the front, with other information and messages on the back.

Use cheerful colors. The bear fur, the house and the roof are painted as washes, using a flat or round brush well loaded with diluted color. Darker areas are achieved by going over the same spot with more diluted color. You can add other colors for interesting shading. Tree leaves are stippled on with the chisel point of a flat brush. Remember to hold the brush in a vertical position for this effect. Use a round brush for the roses and leaves on the border. Your detail brush will do the rest. See Fig. 6-1 for a guideline drawing.

Commemorative Project #2: Wedding Pitcher

There are many pitchers available in greenware: small, large, straight up and down, rounded, contemporary and traditional. A floral design incorporating names

FIG. 6-1 Guideline drawing for Baby Plate project. As with all drawings, copy free-hand, making any changes you desire, or enlarge, trace, and transfer.

and wedding date will work well on most shapes and will be a lovely way to commemorate this special day. If you know the china pattern chosen by the bride you can include some of those colors. If you don't, you will find a blue border to be a safe bet.

If the location of their wedding is important to them, add that too. And don't forget to write your good wishes on the bottom. The pitcher design in Fig. 6-2 uses

FIG. 6-2 Guideline drawing for Wedding Pitcher project.

This group of ceramic pieces shows the delightful work that children can create. These items were painted by my children Caitlin and Timothy, when they were between the ages of four and eleven. The key to their charm is the natural and spontaneous use of color.

Photo by David Allison

Children paint easily and naturally on tiles, finding the size and shape comfortable to work on. The tile with the imaginative abstract design was painted by eleven-year-old Josh Merin, the others by my young daughter, Caitlin.

Photo by David Allison

These dinner plates were the first ceramic paintings done by Diane Herbort. They were inspired by her collection of old Christmas cards and books. Her style reflects the many drawings she has done as needlework and quilt designer and author.

Photo by David Allison

Ceramics, in relief or three-dimensional, are as interesting a medium of self-expression as painting or sculpture. The relief is by the Italian ceramist DeSimone. The vase is mine.

Photo by David Allison

These four tiles show the stages of painting. *Top left* is the initial sketch; *top right,* the painted tile. *Bottom left,* the colors are fired in and the pencil marks disappear. *Bottom right,* the finished, glazed and re-fired tile. *Photo by David Allison*

Simple floral tiles and handpainted articles can add warmth and sparkle to a plain, small kitchen.

Photos by David Allison

Here are some simple designs you can try on tiles. (See "Decorative Project #2" in Chapter 6.) Combine the corner, border and individual designs as you wish, then add your own.

This is the baby plate used as the practice piece. *Photo by David Allison*

A baby plate that you can personalize in your own way. (See "Commemorative Project #1" in Chapter 6.)
Photo by David Allison

Another house portrait, this time on a plate, makes the best "thank you" gift.
Photo by David Allison

A house portrait done on tiles, based on photographs or drawings, is a wonderful way to immortalize a special place. (See "Commemorative Project #3" in Chapter 6.) *Photo by David Allison*

Tile scene set into a table for indoor or outdoor use.
Photo by Donna Cantor

An asymmetric floral design adds appeal to a large oval "basket" that can be used as a platter or tray. The outside surface is also decorated.

This abstract design on a platter is a wonderful exercise in painting pressure strokes and squiggles. (See "Decorative Project #3" in Chapter 6.) I have used primarily opaque underglazes, putting light highlights over darker areas. Although the design itself is quite different, the colors and the mood complement the Collier and Campbell fabric.

a simple rose with a blue border and blue lettering. I have used two greens for the leaves and stems, and a light pink with dark rose accents and outlines for the roses. You will need your liner, round and detail brushes.

Commemorative Project #3: House Portrait on Tiles

Tiles can be used as murals, pictures to be framed or in a table or tray.

Scenes work well on horizontal rectangles, so I suggest painting on twelve tiles (4 by 3) or twenty tiles (5 by 4). The first thing you must do is number the tiles on the back with the underglaze pencil. (The numbers won't fire out.) Then lay them out close together in numerical order, as in Fig. 6-3.

These tiles are your canvas, and you will be drawing across all of them. Use a drawing (yours or someone else's) or a photograph of the house as your model.

FIG. 6-3   These twelve tiles are laid out horizontally in three rows, with four tiles in each row.

1	2	3	4
5	6	7	8
9	10	11	12

You can, of course, draw free-hand a sketch of the house onto the tiles. For a more exact rendition, trace the outline of the house, including placement of windows and doors, from the photograph or drawing. You can now reduce or enlarge this tracing to the exact size you need on the tiles with the help of a copy machine. When you have the right size, transfer it to the tiles by using the techniques described in Chapter 2. Use your imagination when you add the other details. You can improve on the landscape design, by moving trees and flowers to better places, putting them behind light color houses for contrast, or in front of plain houses. Add people or animals, mailboxes or flower pots. Personalize it with the house number or family name on the door. Add a border design and incorporate a family name or date into it. Then sign your painting in the lower right hand corner, just like the artist that you are. See Fig. 6-4 for guideline drawing.

You can use all your brushes for this project, though you will primarily need the flat brush and the detail brush. Your flat brush will be used for all the large areas as well as the tree foliage. For foliage you can use the ragged chisel points of worn

FIG. 6-4 Guideline drawing for the House Portrait project. You can use it for practice, or substitute a house more meaningful to you. You can draw free-hand or trace from a photograph and transfer.

out brushes to good effect. Holding the brush in a vertical position, stipple the leaves or pine needles with your chisel point. You can alternate different greens, or be even more adventurous and add other colors too. Touches of yellow, pink, lilac and blue will give an impressionist touch to your trees. A lilac or washy purple makes wonderful shading, and light blue accents on the windows give the impression of glass. Use washes of one or two blues for the sky.

Decorative Project #1: Place Setting

Design your own dishes and impress your guests! The drawings in Fig. 6-5 show how one general pattern can be used on a plate, bowl, cup and saucer. After you try these, you will find it easy to adapt a pattern to all the pieces that make up a set of dishes, no matter what their size or shape. This is a wonderful project, that you will enjoy adding to. Start with a basic place setting and then add interesting serving dishes as you find them. Don't try to make all the dishes look exactly the same. You don't want them to look manufactured. Some of the variations that are possible are:

* Keep the pattern the same but change the border color.

* Keep the border the same but change the pattern.

* Use basically the same border and pattern, but change just the center flowers or colors.

The design in Fig. 6-5 is a simple floral. Use your liner brush for the stems, and your round brush for the petals and leaves. The flat brush is used for the blue border.

Decorative Project #2: Tiles

Try just a few tiles at first and make small objects. Then paint more and become your own interior decorator.

The tiles in this section can be used individually, or in small or large groups, and can be permanently installed in your house. The designs are repeatable and

plate design

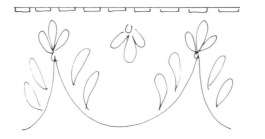

exterior design for bowl

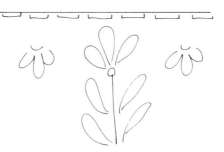

exterior design for cup

FIG. 6-5 Guideline drawings for a dinnerware Place Setting project.

saucer design

interior design for bowl

can be used in combination. For instance, as a splashback in a kitchen or bath-room the border design can be the top row, with a sprinkling of individual tiles underneath. On a work island counter top four corner designs and individual designs can be combined, whereas on a countertop that butts up to a tiled wall it might be more appropriate to combine all three elements. There is no limit to the area you can cover.

For the designs pictured in Fig. 6-6 you will use your liner, round and detail brushes. You can, if you like, use the chisel point of your flat brush for pressure strokes too.

Tiles with Corner Design

This corner design in Figs. 6-6, 6-7 and 6-8 is very versatile. It can be reduced to cover one tile, enlarged to cover eight or twelve tiles, or reversed and then repeated. Repeated in all four corners it becomes a border for a table, or a kitchen counter. As a practice project, take one corner design and combine with blank tiles. Mount them on a piece of plywood or masonite, frame it, add a grease pencil and you will have a lovely message board.

Tiles with Border Design

This repeatable design in Fig. 6-7 is usable as a border on a backsplash. It can be used as the top row, bottom row or anywhere between. It can be repeated endlessly for as long as you need it, or it can end on either side with the corner design. Four corner designs and the border designs will, of course, form a frame design.

Tiles with Repeat Design

The four individual tiles in Fig. 6-8, each with a different flower, can be repeated any number of times. How they are repeated will be the main factor in creating the overall design. The painted tiles can be interspersed with blank tiles for a lighter look, as in Fig. 6-9, or combined in varying order as in Fig. 6-10.

Text continued on page 94

FIG. 6-6 Guideline drawing for corner design.

FIG. 6-7 Guideline drawing for border design.

FIG. 6-8 Guideline drawings for repeat designs.

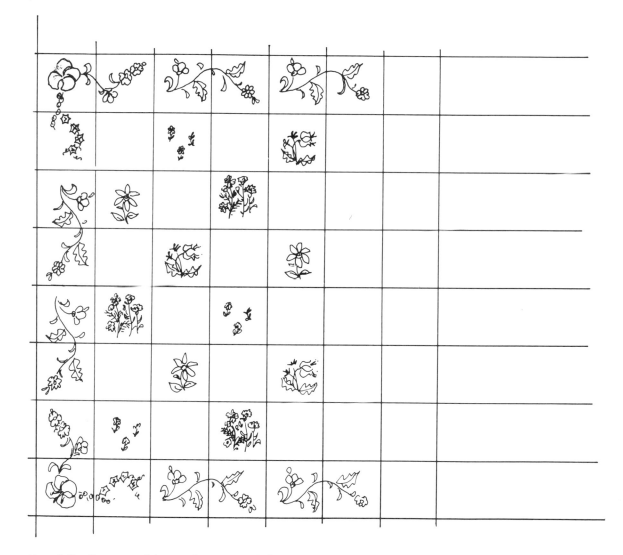

FIG. 6-9 One possible combination of the various tile designs. Corner and border designs frame the pattern made up of individual handpainted and blank tiles. You can vary the interior pattern by changing colors, having more blank tiles, using only one or two of the individual designs, turning some of the designs sideways or upside-down, etc.

FIG. 6-10 Another possible tile combination using the same designs. Corner and border designs frame a small area within a field of tiles decorated with the small flower pattern. Parts of the corner design are used as individual tiles. Designs are reversed or turned upside-down when desired. Colors can vary even if design doesn't. There are endless possibilities.

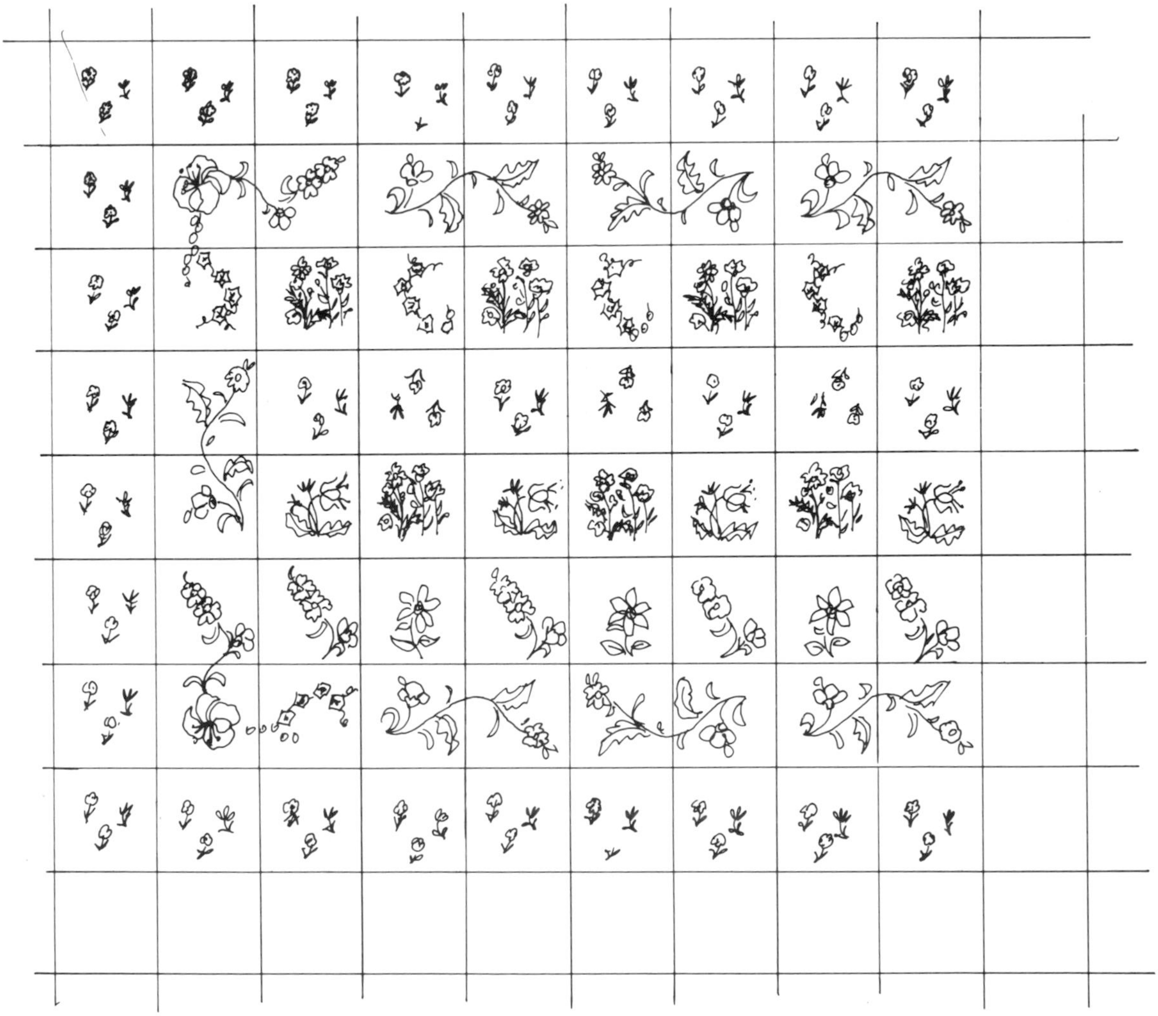

FIG. 6-11 Guideline drawing for Abstract Platter project.

They can be installed with the stem and flower in varying directions (upside down or sideways), generating a feeling of movement and energy; or the flowers can be orderly and well mannered and stand quietly in rows. These tiles can also be combined with the border design and/or the corner design.

FIG. 6-12 Trace design elements from fabric. Use the tracing to figure out their placement on the lamp base. Then free-hand draw them onto the lamp base or transfer from the tracing. *Photo by David Allison*

Decorative Project #3: Platter

An abstract design can be very striking on a large piece like this. Free and easy is the formula here. Use a combination of opaque and translucent underglazes, and be fanciful. Add squiggles and dots to larger areas of colors. You have a great opportunity to practice all your brushstrokes. A dark translucent color will work well over a larger area of opaque color. If you want light touches over darker areas, use one-stroke opaque underglazes. Fabrics and sheets may give you some wonderful ideas for these designs. The design provided in Fig. 6-11 is easier than it looks. The pattern here is just a few basic preset shapes. To these, add as many brushstrokes and squiggles as you like, making a simple design or an intricate one. No drawing skills are required—you can just experiment and have fun.

Decorative Project #4: Lamp Base

This project is different from the others in that you will be creating this design to complement and coordinate with fabric that you have chosen. You can add a plain shade or decorate that too.

Since this is a true interior decoration item, your lamp base should be designed to fit comfortably into your room's decor. As with all well-chosen accessories it can help create just the look and atmosphere you like.

You can trace and copy the fabric design, adapting it to the shape of the lamp base. Or you can take the fabric as inspiration, using only colors and elements of the design, and create your own pattern. Remember that tracing paper and your local copy machine can be very useful in copying, enlarging, reducing and transferring the design elements you want to use.

The fabric I have chosen here is easy to translate to ceramics. The colors are similar to those available in underglazes. I simplified the petal shapes to be simple pressure strokes. See Fig. 6-12.

Be creative and have fun!

*I*n the preceding chapters I have mentioned many products and books, and in this section I would like to provide additional information as well as sources. I would enjoy hearing from you about any additional discoveries you may make.

Ceramic Supplies

Ceramic supplies are as near as the ceramics listing in your yellow pages. Ceramics is a very popular hobby and you should have no trouble locating all the supplies you need. There are also many large mail-order suppliers, and firing can be done wherever there is a kiln: a school or community center, for instance.

Don't forget a hint I gave you earlier in the book. Large ceramic shows will often have distributors selling at wholesale prices. Take advantage of these prices to buy major equipment or to stock up on glaze and brushes. Don't stock up too much on underglazes, for they have the tendency to dry up, even if not used. Hobby ceramics magazines (I've listed some in the following pages) publish calendars of these shows, and your local ceramic shops will usually post notices of shows in your area. Shows also offer you the chance to enter your creations in competitions.

Greenware and Bisque

Greenware is available through local ceramic shops. Distributors, who sell to the small shops, will often deal directly with the public also. Generally, the price of a piece of greenware is 10% of the cost of the mold. Thus small, simple pieces will be cheaper than large, hard-to-pour ones. If a handle has to be poured separately and then attached, it is more expensive because it takes more time. Firing usually costs 50% of the cost of the greenware. In short, if a mold costs $25, each piece of greenware will cost $2.50 and each firing $1.25. If you don't want to clean your own greenware the shop will do that too, at an additional charge—often the cost of a firing.

Ceramic shops will have many molds that they don't always pour, so make sure to ask if you are looking for something specific. Ask your shop to show you mold catalogues, so you can see what is available. Hobby ceramic magazines are useful for showing you what new molds and supplies are available. Ceramic shops will also have "out-of-print" molds too, as long as they are still in good condition. (Molds are made of plaster and do get damaged with repeated use.)

You can, of course, make your own molds. This is practical only if you want to produce large quantities of each design and requires an investment in equipment, as well as studio space. It is certainly not the solution for everyone, but if you want to explore the possibility of designing and making your own molds for production work, the best guidance you'll find is Donald Frith's *Mold Making for Ceramics* (Chilton, 1985). Bound into the book are a plaster batch calculator and a shrinkage compensating calculator, extremely helpful to the production potter.

If there is a special shape or item you absolutely must have but cannot find an appropriate mold for, ask your local potter. This will probably cost you more than slipcast greenware, but it will be worth it. Remember to specify low-fire clay.

I had hoped, once I was in business and needed dishes by the dozen, to be able to skip the greenware (unfired clay) stage completely and just find a source willing to give me already cleaned and fired bisque at bulk prices. A china company, I thought, which should be easy to find—but it wasn't. I found out that Wheaton Glass' china factory wasn't the only one to close. American china companies are in such competition with foreign companies that they can no longer afford to manufacture china that has the bisque-for-decoration stage. China is now automatically manufactured and glazed in one step to minimize hand labor. Decoration is normally applied as decals on the glazed ware or sometimes silk-screened, as on mugs. I did have a source—briefly—but it didn't last, succumbing to financial pressure as other companies did. Oh, well, maybe someday . . .

Meanwhile, greenware provides a great variety of articles, and does not need to be ordered in bulk. Your local ceramic shop will also clean and fire it for you, if you wish.

Tiles

Handcast tiles are available in greenware at ceramic shops, but I prefer the more durable and uniform commercially made bisque tiles available from tile distributors. These are generally sold by the box and are much less expensive than handcast ones. Your yellow pages can help you locate sources. Summitville and American Olean are two possible sources. I recommend using 4″ rather than 6″ tiles. The 6″ tiles have a tendency to break in the firing, *after* you've painted them. If you are planning to match your handpainted tiles to already existing tiles, or want to combine them with standard, blank, glazed tiles, be sure to measure carefully. Each manufacturer's "standard" size is slightly different, even in thickness. Also please note that standard glazed tiles are coated with opaque glazes, rather than clear glaze over bisque. You will want a color closest to your bisque color. There will be many shades of white and almond to choose from.

Brushes

Brushes are available at ceramic shops, art supply stores and ceramic shows. Experiment until you find the ones just right for you. Be sure to buy good quality brushes. Sable, sabeline and Taklon work especially well. Make sure bristles come to a nice clean point or smooth chisel end, and then take good care to keep them that way. Scraggly brushes can't make good brushstrokes. Also detail brushes tend to wear out, so once you have discovered a brand you like you may be interested in buying them by the dozen at ceramic shows. When buying glaze brushes you will be especially interested in a brush that doesn't shed bristles.

Tools

Tools are available at ceramic shops, potters' supply houses and ceramic shows.

Underglazes, Glazes and Overglazes

Several major companies produce a variety of underglazes and glazes. Normally, small shops just handle one or two brands, but larger suppliers will be able to provide various brands. Not every company makes the same colors, so again be sure to experiment. You will enjoy putting together a palette of your favorite colors. The following list of manufacturers and products I have found to be especially useful.

Duncan Enterprises
5673 E. Shields Avenue
Fresno, CA 93727

Duncan manufactures a wide variety of ceramic products—primarily for hobby ceramists—from colors and brushes to molds and kilns. These products are easily available through dealers and distributors.

The EZ-Strokes line of translucent, concentrated underglazes offers the widest variety of colors that I have found on the market. Most of them go very well with each other. Because they are translucent, they can be used much like watercolors. I use mostly EZ-Strokes.

The Design Coats line of colors can be used as one or two coat colors for semi-opaque or opaque coverage. They are thicker and less controllable than EZ-

Strokes and therefore less suited for fine detail work. But their color selection is nice, and their opacity is good for larger area coverage. They are good to use in combination with EZ-Strokes.

The Cover Coats line is for large and opaque area coverage. Three coats are required. I personally don't use them often, though I do like to use the flesh colors. Because of their true opacity, no streaking occurs.

Gloss Glazes are available in many colors, translucent, semi-translucent, semi-opaque and opaque. For the purposes of this book we need only one: GL 611 Ultraclear (food-safe clear glaze). It is available in 4-ounce, pint and gallon containers. Clearly, the gallon size is most cost-effective for it will keep.

> *American Art Clay Company (AMACO)*
> *4717 W. 16th Street*
> *Indianapolis, IN 46222-2598*

AMACO ceramic products are geared toward potters rather than hobby ceramists, but you will find many products you can use: brushes, transfer paper, tools, colors, glazes, kilns and books. Their catalogue is beautiful, filled with photographs of the work of imaginative potters. You will be eager to add it to your idea library. AMACO is a very accessible company with a real commitment to education.

I have found these unique products especially interesting:

Semi-moist Underglaze Decorating Colors. These come in sets of 8 pans of colors, like a watercolor set. Concentrated and opaque, they are easy to use, smooth on the brush and good for fine detail.

Underglaze Decorating Pencils, available in black, brown, blue, green, rose and yellow. I find the black and brown pencils the most useful. They can be used for shading and drawing, and for outlining when a softer line is desired. I find them especially effective for architectural outlines and details; for animal fur and hair; and for identification (numbering tiles on the back, having students put their names on the underside of their work, etc.).

Underglaze Decorating Chalk Crayons to create the effect of pastels. Harder to use than underglazes, but worth knowing about.

Gare, Inc.
165 Rosemount Street
Haverhill, MA 01831
(617) 373-9131

Gare is another large manufacturer of hobby ceramic products, including colors, molds and kilns. Products are easily available through dealers and distributors.

Olevia Color, Inc.
Scotia-Glenville Industrial Park
Scotia, NY 12302
(800) 234-5654

These colors may be ordered directly from the manufacturer, since they are hard to find in supply houses. You will enjoy adding some of their colors to your palette. Their translucent, concentrated underglazes are called Detail Strokes and really are very effective for detail work.

Ceramichrome Inc.
P.O. Box 327
Stanford, KY 40484
(606) 365-3193

Ceramichrome products are relatively easy to obtain from dealers and distributors. Their Detail One-Stroke Opaque Underglazes are especially interesting. Because they are opaque: the colors are sometimes more intense than their equivalents in translucent underglazes; they don't fade out as easily; and, light colors can be painted over darker ones. They are also more suited for very fine detail than Duncan's Design Coats. The color I have used most often is Ming Blue.

Kilns

Buy a kiln that can be easily serviced, is easy to use and is as foolproof as possible. Duncan and Gare kilns are especially made for hobbyists, and are easily available from many local distributors. Skutt and AMACO kilns are also highly recommended.

When your local ceramic shop can't find what you want, tell them about this wholesale ceramics supply distributor and have them send for a catalogue:

Creative Hobbies Inc.
900 Creek Road
Bellmawr, NJ 08031-1687
(800) THE-KILN

Creative Hobbies sells all kinds of ceramic products and publications by a wide variety of manufacturers. They deal only with the trade, so you will have to have your local shop order for you.

Reference Materials

You can use these materials to start your idea library. You will find yourself lending them out to all your other creative friends looking for inspiration.

Books

Ceramic and Pottery Books—how-to books are best found in pottery and ceramic supply stores, but histories of ceramics, porcelain and pottery are also available in bookstores, along with art books. Be sure to look through remainders and sale books. You will find the decoration of dishes and tiles of most interest to you.

Two books I especially like are: *Country Floors: Decorating with Tiles* by Roslyn Siegel (New York, NY: Simon and Schuster, 1989) and *Contemporary Pottery Decoration* by John Gibson (Radnor, PA: Chilton Books, 1988).

Art and Design Books—an endless source of design ideas. Remember to look through all manifestations of design: painting, graphics and advertising, textile design, quilts and embroidery, to name just a few. Period books (e.g., art deco, art nouveau, Victorian, Wiener Werkstaette, etc.) can be very helpful for they demonstrate how design elements cross media lines. Learn to browse through the unfamiliar for there may be styles you don't recognize by name, but which would help you in designing.

Don't forget to look for books about artists and how they work and think about their art. I especially recommend: *The Art of Zandra Rhodes* (Boston, MA: Houghton Mifflin Company, 1985) and *Carl Larsson's Home* (Reading, MA: Addison-Wesley Publishing Company, 1981).

Dover Books—Dover Publications of New York is a wonderful publisher! Their books are inexpensive and cover such a wide variety of subjects that you will always find one more you want. Their books are available in book stores and art supply stores, but since no one store carries all their books you will do well to send for a free catalogue. You can then order by mail. Their titles are usually self-explanatory, and you can count on their good quality. Four specific Dover books that I have used often are: *1001 Spot Illustrations of the Lively Twenties, The Spectacular Floral Designs of E.A. Seguy, Benedictus' Art Deco Designs,* and *400 Floral Motifs for Designers, Needleworkers and Craftspeople* (edited by Carol Belanger Grafton). You can write to Dover at:

Dover Publications Inc.
180 Varick Street
New York, NY 10014

Children's books—if you saved your own, or have children, you probably already have many that you can use. Children's books from the 20s and 30s often have lovely illustrations. Discount book stores are also a good source of children's books, as are yard sales and flea markets. Remember, this time it's the pictures not the story that count.

A must is Beatrix Potter—any edition will do. And don't overlook *Richard Scarry's Best Word Book Ever* (New York, NY: Golden Press, 1963).

Nature books—these are very helpful for those scenes you will paint on tiles and dishes. You can use books geared toward children or field guides. It makes things easy if you have a library ready at hand with pictures of anything you might need: mammals, birds, fish, trees, flowers, seashells and people. Bookstores often have sale books and remainders for this part of your collection. My favorite nature book is *The Backyard Bestiary* illustrated by Kees de Kiefte (New York, NY: Alfred A. Knopf, 1982).

Magazines

There are several ceramics magazines on the market. You will find them very useful for product and show information. They offer specific projects for you to transfer and copy, and will give you very specific instructions on how to execute them. I find that although their projects involve painting and surface design, they are not oriented toward painting as a means of self-expression. If you do try some of the projects, then be sure to inject your own personality by making changes and making your own decisions as to color. You may actually find artists' magazines more inspiring. Needlework magazines often have lovely designs, and I think it is more creative to adapt a design in your way to your medium than it is to just paint-by-number. It is also worthwhile looking at decorating magazines to see how ceramics are used as a decorating element.

Ceramics
P.O. Box 1968
Marion, OH 43305

A hobby ceramics magazine, catering especially to novices starting off in pottery.

Ceramic Showcase
165 Rosemont Street
P.O. Box 1686
Haverhill, MA 01831

A hobby ceramics magazine published by Gare Inc.

Popular Ceramics
P.O. Box 6466
Glendale, CA 91205-9990

A magazine of ceramics projects with many helpful advertisements and show calendars.

Ceramics Arts and Crafts Magazine
30595 West 8 Mile Road
Livonia, MI 48152

A hobby ceramics magazine with lots of easy projects and suggestions for novices.

Ceramics Monthly
Box 12448
Columbus, OH 43212

This is a quality magazine directed primarily toward potters, but it is interesting to see how potters approach pottery decoration. It's generally quite different than hobby ceramics.

McCalls Needlework and Crafts
P.O. Box 10787
Des Moines, IA 50349

I have designed and written several how-to features for this magazine. Although geared primarily toward needlework, its strength lies in showing the interaction and complementary nature of crafts, and how one type of design can have various applications. The magazine is good inspiration.

House Beautiful
Box 10083
Des Moines, IA 50350

A beautiful home decorating and style magazine, with ideas that are accessible or at least inspirational to an average person.

Creative Ideas for Living
810 *Seventh Avenue*
New York, NY 10019

A decorating magazine that emphasizes using crafts, preferably your own, to personalize your surroundings.

Country Home
P.O. Box 10667
Des Moines, IA 50336

A country style decorating magazine in which handpainted ceramics would certainly feel at home.

Country Living (*the British edition*)
72 *Broadwick Street*
London WIV 2BP *England*

This is a decorating and lifestyle magazine of real beauty and quality and is my favorite. It will show you many ways to incorporate ceramics into your home. The features on other crafts and on gardens will also give you many design ideas. It is available by subscription for about $40 per year airmail. You may also find single issues in bookstores that carry foreign magazines and newspapers.

American Craft
40 *West 53rd Street*
New York, NY 10019

Published by the American Craft Council (ACC). A subscription to this bi-monthly publication includes ACC membership, free admission to the American

Craft Museum in New York, research privileges at their library, discounts, etc. Articles feature the best in American crafts.

Add to your library anything you find helpful. Things to keep your eyes open for are:

Greeting Cards and Note Cards

Museums and book stores often offer the best and most interesting selection. Many of these can be obtained by mail. Especially interesting catalogues are offered by the following museums.

The Metropolitan Museum of Art
Fifth Avenue
New York, NY 10017

Boston Museum of Fine Arts
P.O. Box 1044
Boston, MA 02120

Smithsonian Institution
Washington, D.C. 20560

Gift Wrap

Wonderful gift wraps are being printed these days: new and original designs as well as reproductions of lovely old fabrics, wallpapers, marbled papers, quilts, etc. Florentine and Japanese rice papers are also beautiful. Look for them in card shops, museum shops, catalogues and book stores.

Art Calendars

Look at art calendars as less expensive art books. If you wait until spring you can often buy them half-price. European ones are especially nice, and they print many small, inexpensive calendars.

Fabric and Wallpaper Samples

You can always borrow these books from fabric and wallpaper stores, and then make some sketches. Sometimes shop owners will let you have the discontinued books. If you know any interior designers, ask them if they can help you get some.

Craft Business Sources

If you become so interested in your new hobby that you decide to make a career of it, or if you are already a craftsperson, I highly recommend an interesting and very useful publication:

> The Crafts Report
> (A *Newsmonthly of Marketing, Management and Money*
> *for Crafts Professionals*)
> 700 Orange Street
> Wilmington, DE 19801

I also recommend a book by the editor of *The Crafts Report, The Crafts Business Encyclopedia: Marketing, Management, and Money* by Michael Scott (New York, NY: Harcourt Brace Jovanovich, 1979), which is available for $5.95 plus $.95 for shipping and handling from:

> The Crafts Report *Book Dept.*
> Box 1992
> Wilmington, DE 19899

Inexpensive business cards, stationery and stickers are available through Walter Drake's mail-order catalogue.

> Walter Drake
> 59 Drake Bldg.
> Colorado Springs, CO 80940

Large quantities of business cards, postcard size, with photograph(s) can be ordered from:

> Mitchell Color Cards
> 2230 E. Mitchell
> Petoskey, MI 49770
> (800) 841-6793

Last but not least I would like to recommend the work of two experts in their field. First, the photographer of most of the photographs in this book:

> David Allison
> 3605 Norris Place
> Alexandria, VA 22305

Mr. Allison's specialty is photographing art collections, artifacts and documents. He has done extensive work for the Smithsonian, National Archives and other museums as well as private clients. His own fine-art photographs are exhibited in several museums and collections in the United States and abroad. His wife is an artist, so he is sympathetic to other artists' financial constraints.

Next, when it comes time for you, your friends or your clients, to install your handpainted tiles, you'll find no one better than:

> Terry Millar
> Geo Tile and Marble
> 6802 Kincaid Avenue
> Falls Church, VA 22042
> (703) 534-5537

*T*ime has passed. You have mastered the art of painting on ceramics. Innumerable ideas form in your mind and flow out through your brush, but you can't justify making yourself so many things, and there is a limit to how often you can give gifts! You can't stop! What to do? It's time to become an entrepreneur!

To get started you will want to decide what you are going to sell, where you will sell it, and how you will sell it. There are many books at the library that can help you, and I've outlined some of the things I've learned. Remember to get a business license and tax number.

What To Sell

If you are always filled with ideas and don't like doing the same things all the time then you will probably enjoy doing custom and personalized work. If, on the other hand, you don't mind repetition, and get pleasure out of seeing twenty of your designs lined up on your shelf, then production work may be for you. There are pros and cons to both, and you will probably want to do a combination of the two. Custom work needs only an audience of one at a time. Production work has to appeal to a broad range of people. With my own work I have found that generally my florals are standard, production work; whereas scenes are usually personal and customized. It is a good balance for me. Tile work is usually custom work no matter what the design.

Custom designed and personalized items that sell especially well are:

* baby gifts (usually plates, bowls and mugs)

* wedding and anniversary gifts (usually platters, pitchers and bowls)

* Christmas gifts

* thank you gifts for teachers, coaches, nurses, school bus drivers and others who have performed kindnesses and services (generally mugs or plates)

* house portraits (normally on tiles or platters)

* any occasion for which you cannot easily find ready made gifts

* door plaques and other signs

* sets of dishes

* dog and cat bowls

Production items that I have generally decorated with floral designs and that have worked well for me are:

* bowls

* pitchers

* platters

* candlesticks

* baskets

* planters

* door plaques (standard words, not personalized)

* Christmas ornaments

Where to Sell

There is always a market for the beautiful and practical. And in this high-tech, computerized age there is certainly a market for the personal. How do you find this market? I started by making things for friends, of course, but the first attempt at "marketing" was a Tupperware-style party in which a friend invited other friends to see my wares. A party like this can show the work of several artists or craftspeople at the same time. In return for giving the party, you can give your friend a custom designed and handpainted gift. Other parties will certainly follow as a result. It is also the beginning of never-ending word-of-mouth contacts. Happy recipients make the best customers. And happy recipients of custom designs become repeat customers. You will find it easy and natural to establish a very pleasant relationship with customers for whom you do custom work and with whom you deal directly. It comes from having to communicate ideas. Soon you will even get long-distance orders, and you will learn how to communicate visual ideas verbally. I have made hundreds of items, including large tile murals, based on telephone conversations.

If you want to sell only once in a while, at your own pace, private customers are the best. You can also sell at craft shows or fairs once in a while. It is a good way to test new ideas. Craft fairs come in all sizes and levels of quality. Determine your products accordingly. Small fairs won't support very high-priced items but small, less expensive items work fine. This does not mean that you should sell your best work cheap. Also consider the season; Christmas ornaments will clearly sell better in the fall than right after New Year's.

If you are interested in long-term, steady work you will probably want to sell to a store. Shop carefully for the right store and the right owners. If you offer custom designed work, the owners need to understand that you are offering a unique service and it is that uniqueness that they need to sell to their customers. The most unique aspect of this custom work is the importance of the customer's input. It is the customer's ideas, memories, events, family, etc. that you will be translating into your designs. The shopowner will have to be able to communicate this to his customers.

The right display, and knowledgeable and friendly sales people are very important. A small store where most items seem unique and lovingly chosen will be the right environment for your work. Custom work should not get lost in a vast assortment of mass-produced souvenirs. If there are no appropriate stores in your area, refer to publications such as *Crafts Report* (see "Resources") which run ads by shops looking for crafts.

If your painting is of especially fine quality, you may be able to sell through art or craft galleries. To test the potential of this market for you it would be a good idea to first enter a few "all media accepted" art competitions. You will probably find resistance to slipcast ware as an acceptable medium, as I did. Don't give up. Explain calmly that a "clay canvas" is equivalent to, and as valid a medium as paper or linen. Furthermore, if the quality of painting is being judged, poured clay is certainly as valid a canvas as thrown clay. A few words about Renaissance maiolica painting won't hurt your cause either. You will be able to overcome this resistance, and next time it won't be so hard.

Serious, Large Quantity Selling

If you want to sell in large quantities you will have to get into production work. You will also have to sell wholesale. Craft cooperatives, large trade shows or agents or sales representatives are the usual ways of attaining the broad exposure needed to sell large quantities. Think carefully before you enter this phase of your career. There are many things you need to know, for there are many things you need to do. Your main concern is the ability to meet your commitments.

To do this:

 ⁕ You must be able to ensure consistent quality.

 ⁕ You must know your production ability, so that you can produce, pack and deliver your product as and when promised.

 ⁕ You must be able to maintain correct and up-to-date accounting and bookkeeping records.

This is a lot for one person to do. So, the decision to wholesale may mean the need to have one or more employees. This, of course, brings other concerns: insurance, social security and paperwork, paperwork.

So, although it sounds wonderful to make more money, be sure you are well informed before you undertake large quantity wholesale. There are many books about running small businesses, especially craft businesses. Read them. You don't want to make commitments you can't meet. If you like tile painting and want architectural type of work you will need to make contact with interior designers and architects. Tile contractors and suppliers can also be of help. Here, again, word-of-mouth can lead to jobs.

If you live in an area where you can set up a shop in your home you have a wide range of possibilities and can try a little of everything. You can work where you sell. You can specialize in custom work or in ready-to-take-with-you, or do both. You can also teach. Start with what you like to do most, then you can expand. Most important, you will have to get your name out so that people will know to come to you.

Good Business Practices

The more professional you are in producing and marketing your work, the more successful you will be, whether you are selling small or large quantities. It's always nice to be considered a quality operation. Your main considerations and concerns as a businessperson are to provide the products you promised when you promised them.

Pricing

Pricing is one of the most difficult aspects of your business. You want your prices to be fair—not only to the consumer but also to yourself. Most beginning artists and craftspeople make the mistake of underpricing their work.

Price certainly reflects costs of materials, overhead and labor, but it is also influenced by the uniqueness and quality of your product, and by the market it targets. High-quality, one-of-a-kind works sold in art or craft galleries can command higher prices than production items sold in craft fairs. Style and location of a store will prompt price adjustments also. If your work is not selling it may be a case of selling to the wrong market rather than selling at the wrong price.

If you are selling in quantity you may want to give quantity discounts. Sets of dishes should cost less than the sum of the individual prices. If you are selling wholesale you will have to keep in mind that the store that sells your work will double the price paid to you. If you are asking $26 wholesale, the retailer will ask $52. You might consider dropping your price to $25, so the store can ask an even $50.

If you are using an agent, you have to include his/her commission in your considerations. You may have to ship your products to stores. This not only costs money for packaging (ceramics are breakable, don't forget) and shipping, but is also a time-consuming job. You will want to add a shipping and handling charge to your price. If you sell retail and wholesale you will have two prices. Be careful not to compete unfairly with your retailer.

Record Keeping

This may be the least enjoyable part of being in business, but it is of great importance. Basically what you want to know, be able to remember, and refer to later is:

What was ordered?—take pictures of your work so that you have a record of all your original ideas. Customers will often want "another one just like . . ." This will help you remember.

Who are your customers?—if you keep records of your customers, you will be able to develop a customer and market profile as well as a mailing list.

What did it cost you, and what did you charge?—costs include all materials needed to produce your piece, utilities, transportation expenses for pick-up and/or delivery, commissions, shipping and packaging, advertising, office supplies and your labor. Costs also include breakage and returns.

What taxes were collected and what taxes were paid?

When was the order received, when did you fill it and when did you receive payment?

Advertising

This entails everything you can and have to do to become known and be remembered.

Have an eye-catching and memorable business card. You can start with a card with a logo to reflect your style. But later, when you can afford it, you'll find that a most effective card is one that is postcard size and has a photograph of your work on one side, and important written information on the other. Hand it out freely. People will keep it and remember you.

For this and other advertising purposes you will probably want to consider having your work professionally photographed. Ask other craftspeople, potters and artists whom they have used. Professional photographers are expensive but usually worth the expense. Photographers sympathetic to artists just starting out will sometimes barter their time for your work.

Put name and address stickers on the bottom of all your work so that recipients (third parties now) will know how to get in touch with you.

Be generous with gifts, offering your work for charity fundraisers and auctions and local public television or radio stations drives. In this way, as many people as possible will hear about you.

Get your local paper interested in your efforts by sending in a press release. The more free advertising you can arrange, the better.

If your work is given as a group gift, then the whole group as well as the recipient will learn about your work.

Teaching Workshops

Spread the good news. I started with children's workshops. Since children are uninhibited about artwork, they just sit down and do it. Children need some technical assistance—how to cream the colors, how to hold the brushes, etc.—but they need little design advice. They are usually full of wonderful ideas. I provided all the supplies and the glazing and firing. A good first project for children is a tile. Once parents saw their children's wonderful creations, they too became interested.

In teaching adults, you have many options: from short "let me just try it" workshops to seminars on design development with complete how-to instructions (this whole book, in other words). You can provide all the materials and do the firing and even the glazing, or let the students arrange these things themselves, or a combination thereof.

Adherence: Ability of a glaze or under-glaze to stay in place on a given surface. Can be affected by oil, dust or salt on bisque surface, or by hardspots caused by over-cleaning greenware, or improper slipcast-ing.

Art pottery: Also called studio pottery; decorative ware made by artist-potters at the end of the nineteenth century.

Bisque: Also known as biscuit. Fired, un-glazed objects of clay. Hard bisque is fired to cone 04 or higher; medium bisque to cone 05; soft bisque to cone 06. If bisque is fired to one or two cones hotter than the glaze firing, it will result in a good, durable sur-face, with less danger of any delayed crazing or thermal shock.

Blistering: Broken bubble on fired glazed surface.

Casting: The process of filling a plaster mold with casting slip, letting it harden with-out pressure, and thereby creating a clay object.

Casting slip: Liquid clay used for casting.

Ceramics: The art and process of making objects out of clay, and then giving them permanent shape by firing in a kiln.

Clay carbon: Carbon-backed paper for transferring designs onto bisque.

Cleaning greenware: Removing mold seam lines, rough areas and imperfections from unfired clay articles.

Cleaning pads: Abrasive pad, usually made of nylon, used to clean greenware.

Cone: Heat-measuring device used when firing a kiln.

Crawling: A glaze defect in which the glaze pulls away from the bisque surface.

Crazing: A network of fine hairline cracks that appears in the glazed surface of a finished ceramic piece. Some crazing is immediate, while some is delayed. Some glazes are developed to craze on purpose, since a uniformly crazed surface can be very attractive. On low-fire ceramics this surface is generally not food-safe.

Creamware: A light-bodied earthenware with transparent (mainly lead-based) glaze; perfected in Staffordshire, England, in about 1740–50, and put into mass-production by Josiah Wedgwood and Thomas Whieldon.

Delftware: Dutch, blue and white, tin-glazed earthenware, named after the town of Delft. By the end of the 16th century the production of maiolica (polychrome tin-glazed earthenware) was established in Haarlem. In the beginning of the 17th century, two shiploads of blue and white Ming porcelain arrived from China. Imitations were undertaken immediately and very quickly polychrome decoration at the Haarlem factory gave way to the blue alone. The shapes became finer to be more like porcelain. The production of blue and white tin-glazed pottery quickly became a national industry, centering in the potteries in Delft. Delftware had a strong influence on the pottery of Northern Europe. (See: Tin-glazed earthenware, Faience, Maiolica, Lustreware)

Detail brush: A very small, round brush with fine point for detailing and lettering.

Double-spiral brush: A double-ended tool with a narrow, straight spiral brush on one end, and a larger, tapered spiral brush on the other; for cleaning greenware.

Dryfooting: Bottom area (foot) left unglazed so that stilting is unnecessary. Usually only done with ceramics that will vitrify. Not recommended for functional low-fire ceramics.

Earthenware. Nonvitreous ware made from low-fire clays. The clay you will be working on.

Elements: Wires in the kiln that carry electrical current for heating.

Faience: Tin-glazed earthenware (maiolica) named for the Italian town of Faenza. Artists in Faenza followed the course of Italian Renaissance art, and developed pictorial representations of classical, mythological and religious scenes on ceramics. Later, a simpler style of maiolica was also developed in Faenza. This tin-glazed earthenware was sold to France and Germany, inspiring development of their own pottery production. French and German "faience" were also greatly influenced by Chinese porcelains and the European version, Delftware. (See: Tin-glazed earthenware, Delftware, Maiolica, Lustreware)

Ferrule: Metal band of brush to hold hair or bristles in place.

Firing: The process of maturing ceramic products by heating in a kiln. The equivalent of baking.

Firing chamber: The inside of a kiln.

Firing cone: (See: Cone)

Flat brush: Brush with flat, chisel-pointed ends. Bristles can be long or short. (The short ones are known as brights in art supply stores.)

Foot: The bottom of a ceramic object. (See: Dryfooting)

Frit: The calcined or partly fused materials of which glass is made; any of various chemically complex glasses used to introduce soluble or unstable ingredients into glazes.

Furniture: (See: Kiln furniture)

Glaze: A fired finish consisting of a prepared mixture of frit, which produces a glass like surface when fired. Glazes can be glossy, matte, or textured; food-safe or lead or cadmium based.

Glaze brush: A brush with full, long hairs for the application of glaze.

Gloss glaze: A glaze that produces a shiny, glass-like finish. Transparent gloss glaze is what is most commonly used over underglaze painting. Tableware requires food-safe gloss glazes.

Greenware: Unfired clay articles.

Grog: Ground up bisque added to clay to reduce shrinkage and add strength; sometimes used to change texture.

Hard spots: Areas on bisque that will reject color or glaze and cause pieces to have bare spots. Sometimes caused by over-sponging greenware, but more often by improper greenware casting (e.g., pouring slip repeatedly in the same spot).

Kiln: A heating chamber for hardening and maturing clay and glaze.

Kiln furniture: Articles such as shelves, posts and stilts, used inside a kiln to stack pottery to be fired.

Kiln gloves: Highly heat-resistant gloves for handling hot kiln and ceramic ware.

Kiln-wash: A coating for the bottom of the kiln, and the kiln shelves, to protect them from glaze drippings.

Lead-free glaze: Food-safe glaze formulated without lead or cadmium compounds.

Leather-hard: Term used to describe clay articles that are damp but hard enough to handle.

Liner brush: Brush with long, pointed hairs for making fine lines.

Loading: Completely filling a brush with color; stacking items in a kiln for firing.

Lustreware: Tin-glazed earthenware that has been decorated with silver or copper oxides over the tin glaze. The technique probably originated in pre-Islamic Egypt and spread to Persia and back to Egypt, reaching a peak of artistry during the Tulunid (868–905) and Fatimid (969–1171) dynasties. During the eighth century, the Moors from North Africa colonized part of the Iberian Peninsula. Hispano-Moresque pottery developed in Andalusia and then migrated to Valencia, which had been conquered from Moors. There began active trade contact between France and Italy, which led to the blossoming of tin-glaze decoration which came to be known as maiolica. (See: Tin-glazed earthenware, Delftware, Maiolica, Faience)

Maiolica: Italian tin-glazed pottery. There had been Italian pottery with painting on tin-glaze since the eleventh century, to which the Crusades then added an Arab influence. In the fifteen century, trade with Valencia brought Hispano-Moresque pottery to Italy. The island of Majorca was on the trade-route and gave its name, maiolica, to the Italian version of the Hispano-Moresque pottery. Under the influence of this pottery, and also the flowering of the Renaissance in Florence, a wide range of motifs and richness of decoration were achieved. Artists in the Italian town of Faenza were pioneers in illustrative painting. The term faience (fayence in Germany) takes its name from this town. The work of all these maiolica potters inspired generations of mass-production potters.

Majolica: During the late eighteenth century, the English potters Wedgwood and Whieldon made fancifully-shaped earthenware using a brown, gold and green "maiolica" palette. In the nineteenth century the term "majolica" was used to describe factory-made, lead-glazed earthenware decorated with bright oxides. Today majolica is often used interchangeably with "maiolica." To remember which is which, just remember that there is no *j* in Italian, so "maiolica" must refer to the Italian techniques.

Maturing point: Temperature needed to mature glaze and clay.

Mold: A hollow plaster of Paris form in which liquid clay (slip) is poured (cast) so as to produce clay articles then called greenware. Molds are reusable, though not indefinitely.

Opaque: Non-transparent, as in glazes and underglazes.

Overglaze: A decorative finish applied onto a glazed surface and then low-fired to make permanent.

Pinholes: Tiny holes in the glaze, a defect caused by under-fired bisque, dust left on ware or in the kiln, applying glaze to greenware, or firing too rapidly.

Porcelain: A translucent clay body maturing at high temperature.

Porosity: The permeability of fired or unfired clay. Bisque is porous, and thus able to absorb decoration applied with underglazes.

Posts: Supports for the kiln shelves.

Pottery: Any article formed from clay.

Pouring: Another term for casting, as in casting molds.

Pyrometer: An instrument that indicates temperature in the kiln.

Pyrometric cone: (See: Cone)

Rolling glaze: Method of covering inside area of ware, by rolling thinned glaze inside, then pouring out excess.

Seam: Ridge formed in greenware where mold pieces are joined.

Shivering: Occurs when the glaze and clay body are incompatible. Usually the clay body shrinks more than the glaze, causing the glaze to peel.

Shrinkage: Reduction in the size of a clay object as a result of firing, during which moisture is removed.

Slip: Clay in liquid form.

Stack: Load a kiln.

Stilt: Support used to hold a glazed article above the kiln shelf during firing, so that the glaze does not stick to the shelf.

Stoneware: A heavily grogged clay body requiring a high firing to vitrify.

Terracotta: Natural low-fired clay. Also used to denote the color of that clay.

Thermal shock: The effect on clay articles or glaze caused by abrupt changes in temperature.

Tin-glazed earthenware: Tin-glazed pottery had already been known in the ancient near East, and by the ninth century A.D. it was widely established. Fired earthenware is dipped in or coated with a suspension of lead glaze made opaque by the addition of tin oxide. The porous body absorbs the water, and the glaze is left in an even deposit over the surface. Decoration is then painted on this white deposit. Tin-glazed earthenware was made to emulate the fine porcelains from China, and accounts for most of the luxury ceramics in Europe until Boettger discovered the secret of porcelain in Meissen, Germany in the early eighteenth century. (See: Delftware, Faience, Lustreware, Maiolica)

Translucent: Transparent, allowing light to show through (as in porcelain) or color underneath to show (as in underglazes).

Underglaze: A ceramic color used to paint under a glaze. Concentrated underglazes require only one coat, others two or three. Underglazes can be translucent or opaque.

Vitreous: Impervious to moisture; glass-like.

Vitrify: To become stone-hard and impervious to moisture. High-fire clays vitrify, low-fire clays do not.

Index